W9-CDN-199

Date Due

BUILDING
HISTORY
SERIES

THE
VIKING
LONGSHIP

TITLES IN THE BUILDING HISTORY SERIES INCLUDE:

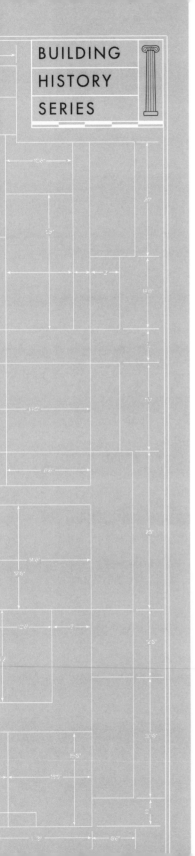

BUILDING
HISTORY
SERIES

THE
VIKING
LONGSHIP

by Lynda Trent

Lucent Books, Inc., San Diego, California

Library of Congress Cataloging-in-Publication Data

Trent, Lynda, 1942–
    The Viking longship / by Lynda Trent.
        p.   cm. — (The building history series)
    Includes bibliographical references and index.
    Summary: Describes the history and culture of the Vikings
and attributes much of their exploring and raiding success to
the well-designed longship.
    ISBN 1-56006-443-9 (lib. : alk. paper)
    1. Vikings—Juvenile literature.   2. Viking ships—Juvenile
literature. [1. Vikings.   2. Ships.]   I. Title.   II. Series.
DL65.T74   1999
948'.022—dc21   98-30360
                                                                    CIP
                                                                    AC

Copyright 1999 by Lucent Books, Inc.
P.O. Box 289011, San Diego, California, 92198-9011

Printed in the U.S.A.

CONTENTS

⚏ FOREWORD

Throughout history, as civilizations have evolved and prospered, each has produced unique buildings and architectural styles. Combining the need for both utility and artistic expression, a society's buildings, particularly its large-scale public structures, often reflect the individual character traits that distinguish it from other societies. In a very real sense, then, buildings express a society's values and unique characteristics in tangible form. As scholar Anita Abramovitz comments in her book *People and Spaces*, "Our ways of living and thinking—our habits, needs, fear of enemies, aspirations, materialistic concerns, and religious beliefs—have influenced the kinds of spaces that we build and that later surround and include us."

That specific types and styles of structures constitute an outward expression of the spirit of an individual people or era can be seen in the diverse ways that various societies have built palaces, fortresses, tombs, churches, government buildings, sports arenas, public works, and other such monuments. The ancient Greeks, for instance, were a supremely rational people who originated Western philosophy and science, including the atomic theory and the realization that the earth is a sphere. Their public buildings, epitomized by Athens's magnificent Parthenon temple, were equally rational, emphasizing order, harmony, reason, and above all, restraint.

By contrast, the Romans, who conquered and absorbed the Greek lands, were a highly practical people preoccupied with acquiring and wielding power over others. The Romans greatly admired and readily copied elements of Greek architecture, but modified and adapted them to their own needs. "Roman genius was called into action by the enormous practical needs of a world empire," wrote historian Edith Hamilton. "Rome met them magnificently. Buildings tremendous, indomitable, amphitheaters where eighty thousand could watch a spectacle, baths where three thousand could bathe at the same time."

In medieval Europe, God heavily influenced and motivated the people, and religion permeated all aspects of society, molding people's worldviews and guiding their everyday actions. That spiritual mindset is reflected in the most important medieval structure—the Gothic cathedral—which, in a sense, was a model of heavenly cities. As scholar Anne Fremantle so elegantly phrases it, the cathedrals were "harmonious elevations of stone and glass reaching up to heaven to seek and receive the light [of God]."

Our more secular modern age, in contrast, is driven by the realities of a global economy, advanced technology, and mass communications. Responding to the needs of international trade and the growth of cities housing millions of people, today's builders construct engineering marvels, among them towering skyscrapers of steel and glass, mammoth marine canals, and huge and elaborate rapid transit systems, all of which would have left their ancestors, even the Romans, awestruck.

In examining some of humanity's greatest edifices, Lucent Books' Building History series recognizes this close relationship between a society's historical character and its buildings. Each volume in the series begins with a historical sketch of the people who erected the edifice, exploring their major achievements as well as the beliefs, customs, and societal needs that dictated the variety, functions, and styles of their buildings. A detailed explanation of how the selected structure was conceived, designed, and built, to the extent that this information is known, makes up the majority of the volume.

Each volume in the Lucent Building History series also includes several special features that are useful tools for additional research. A chronology of important dates gives students an overview, at a glance, of the evolution and use of the structure described. Sidebars create a broader context by adding further details on some of the architects, engineers, and construction tools, materials, and methods that made each structure a reality, as well as the social, political, and/or religious leaders and movements that inspired its creation. Useful maps help the reader locate the nations, cities, streets, and individual structures mentioned in the text; and numerous diagrams and pictures illustrate tools and devices that bring to life various stages of construction. Finally, each volume contains two bibliographies, one for student research, the other listing works the author consulted in compiling the book.

Taken as a whole, these volumes, covering diverse ancient and modern structures, constitute not only a valuable research tool, but also a tribute to the human spirit, a fascinating exploration of the dreams, skills, ingenuity, and dogged determination of the great peoples who shaped history.

IMPORTANT DATES IN THE BUILDING OF VIKING LONGSHIPS

820
The first true longship is built at Oseberg.

878
The Danelaw is established on the east coast of England.

793
The first Viking raid takes place at Lindisfarne.

Mid 800s
Vikings colonize Iceland, Faeroes, Hebrides and Orkney islands.

| 750 | 775 | 800 | 825 | 850 | 875 | 900 |

Early 800s
Vikings begin frequent raids on Britain and Europe.

Late 800s
Ottar discovers the northern coast of Europe.

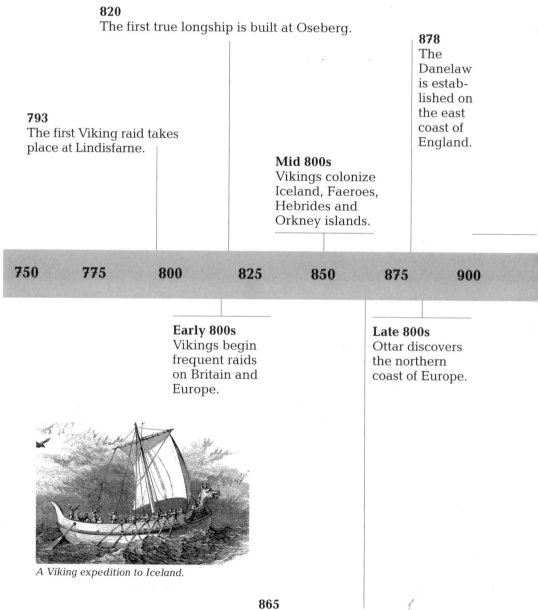

A Viking expedition to Iceland.

865
The Great Army invades England.

A Bayeux Tapestry image depicts the first stages of longship building.

1000
Leif Eriksson discovers North America.

1014
St. Olaf of Norway makes London Bridge fall down.

900s
Greenland is colonized.

925   950   975   1000   1025   1050   1075

1009
First European child, Snorri, is born in America.

1066
William the Conqueror wins the Battle of Hastings, thus taking control of England.

942
Normandy is given to the Vikings in exchange for protection of France.

INTRODUCTION

In about A.D. 787 Europe was shaken to its foundations by a group of people unknown before that time. Three great ships built to resemble fierce dragons heralded their arrivals. They attacked a monastery at Lindisfarne, which was located in Northumbria, the northernmost kingdom of England, killing priests, deacons, monks, nuns, horses, and oxen. Inside the church of St. Cuthbert they killed more priests, dug up the altars, trampled the altar cloths, and stole everything they could find of value, leaving the most holy place in Northumbria bloody and despoiled. Churchmen who were not immediately killed were taken away as slaves or drowned at sea by their captors.

Soon after this, two more raids of equal ferocity took place. One occurred south of Lindisfarne at the monastery at Jarrow. At almost the same time, a third raid was reported on England's southern coast. The attackers had come from different regions of the northernmost reaches of the European continent—primarily Norway, Denmark, and Sweden. All came to be known by the same name: Vikings. With these attacks the Viking era had begun.

The Viking attacks characteristically came without warning. Longships carrying fierce warriors would sweep in silently from the sea to plunder a village, monastery, or farm. The unfortunate villagers or priests would be killed or captured as slaves. Then the longships would vanish as suddenly as they had appeared, leaving no time for the sounding of an alarm or the gathering of defenders to pursue them at sea. Even if a warning was sounded, the Vikings' longships could easily outdistance any of the locally built boats.

COUNTRIES RAIDED BY THE VIKINGS

The Vikings sailed across vast distances in their longships. England, Ireland, and Scotland were just the beginnings. They sailed down the entire western coast of Europe and as far south as the Mediterranean Sea, where they reached Italy, Spain, Morocco, Egypt, and the holy land. Their journeys were not limited to ocean travel. Using rivers, they crossed the continent, reaching Russia, the Black Sea, the Caspian Sea, and Baghdad. In Central Asia they attacked caravans traveling from China. In the Atlantic they reached Iceland, Greenland, and America. Sometimes they plundered and fled; other times, as in Iceland,

For more than 250 years the mere sight of the Viking longship on the horizon was enough to send the occupants of a village into panic.

for example, they established new Viking communities. And they accomplished all of this between the years 793 and about 1066.

People living in countries ranging from the British Isles to Russia came to know and fear the Vikings. No city located near water—and all cities were at that time—was safe from their fearsome raids. Noted historian Gerald Simons describes the Viking attacks:

> Despite fervent prayers for divine deliverance, nothing stayed the Vikings or altered their course. Under reckless and heroic leaders with ominous names—Eric Bloodax, Harald Bluetooth, Ivar the Boneless—they ravaged far and wide. The range and impact of their onslaughts are suggested by the violent visits they paid to towns of Western Europe. Among the dozens of communities that fell to the raiders were towns as far apart as London,

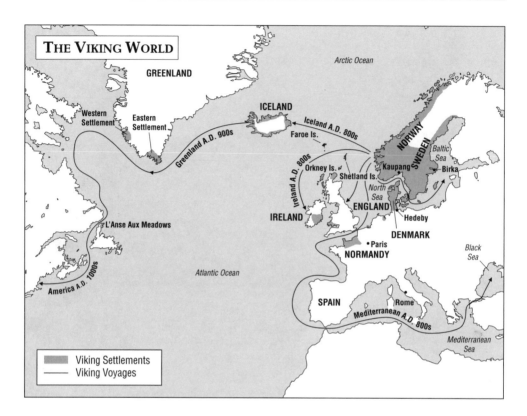

Cadiz and Piza. Viking forces overwhelmed Bordeaux and Paris, captured Rheims and Rouen, sacked and burned Aachen and Cologne. Between 853 and 903 they put Tours to the sword six times.[1]

HOW WE KNOW ABOUT THE VIKINGS

Few facts are known about the longships and the Vikings because they left no written records. Although they had an alphabet made of sticklike characters called runes, they had no paper. To carve the runes onto stones was far too difficult for the recording of history. Parchment did not come to Scandinavia until the middle of the eleventh century, years after the Viking era had passed.

There are four major sources of information about the Vikings. The first source is the sagas they composed, which were long stories about famous Vikings and their adventures as well as about their gods and the myths handed down by earlier generations. These sagas were told around campfires and on long winter nights and were handed down from one generation to the next. People who have no written records learn to memorize in great detail so that an important story will not be lost. Therefore, these sagas were repeated and probably embellished by many generations before they were finally recorded on paper. In the sagas the Vikings appear larger than life and accomplish unimaginable feats.

Another source of knowledge about the Vikings comes from the chronicles and annals of the people they terrorized. Naturally, these accounts are biased; the Vikings are usually described as savage brutes and murderers. Most of these histories

THE VIKING SAGAS

The sagas, which were composed primarily in Iceland—an island discovered and colonized by Vikings—contain a great deal of information about the Vikings. Because Iceland was so isolated from Scandinavia, it was the least affected by other civilizations. In most respects it was a pure Viking community with strong ties to the Norwegian homeland. The sagas were originally handed down by word of mouth and, after pen and paper became available, were written down. They tell the story of events that occurred during the Viking era of raids and colonization, from 793 to about 1066.

Some historians question the accuracy of the sagas, saying that they were meant to entertain and so should not be trusted as a historical record. However, other historians have discovered facts to support the information contained in the sagas. While most were written in the thirteenth century, they are the earliest written accounts that can be attributed to Vikings and their descendants.

The Icelandic sagas are composed of the lives of the Norwegian kings and the Icelandic family sagas. The first claims to give a historical account of all the Norwegian kings from the beginning of history to A.D. 1177. The family sagas are biographies of Icelandic men in the tenth century, many of whom descended from the original Viking colonists. Similar anecdotes can be found in the *Book of the Settlements,* which was written in the early days when the Norwegian Vikings began to colonize Iceland.

A PICTURE STORY TO SHOW HISTORY

One of the most fascinating portrayals of the late Viking era can be seen in a huge pictorial history embroidered in medieval times, probably between 1066 and 1083. The Bayeux Tapestry, which hangs today in the Museum of Queen Matilda at Bayeux in Normandy, France, spans 231 feet in length and 19½ inches in width. It depicts the Norman Conquest of England in 1066, led by William the Conqueror, a direct descendant of the Vikings.

The realistic and detailed portrayal of the Norman Conquest, and the pivotal Battle of Hastings, has led to the Bayeux Tapestry's unique status as both a work of art and a historical document. The Tapestry also contains a running description in Latin of the events it portrays. Although the Norman Conquest of England took place as the Viking era reached its end, historians view the tapestry as a source of information about the Vikings because the story revolves around the direct descendants. The images of warring soldiers, armor, clothing, ships, weapons, and fortifications clearly reflect what is known from other sources about Viking life—both at sea and in battle. The embroidery is so detailed that each horse and each soldier—and even each soldier's shield—differs from the others.

Historians are unsure who designed the tapestry, but they believe it was commissioned by Odo, the bishop of Bayeux and half brother of William the Conqueror.

The Bayeux Tapestry tells the story of the Norman conquest of England. The Normans are direct descendants of the Vikings.

were written by monks—churchmen often being the only ones who had been taught to read and write—and they believed the pagans from the north intended to destroy Christianity.

The Bayeux Tapestry also provides clues about the latter part of the Viking era. This embroidered pictorial history tells the story of the invasion and conquest of England in 1066 by William the Conqueror, who was a direct descendant of the Vikings. Although the Viking era was reaching its end by 1066, the armor, weapons, and ships depicted in detail in the tapestry clearly reflect Viking workmanship and technology.

EVIDENCE LEFT BY THE VIKINGS

The most reliable evidence of Viking life was left by the Vikings themselves—their longships and the relics buried with their dead. As pagans who worshiped many gods, the Vikings believed their dead would need their possessions in the afterlife, so they buried everything that was presumed to be useful. Graves have yielded concrete evidence of armor, weapons, farming tools, and jewelry.

Most important of the grave finds, however, are the burial ships. These were longships that became the coffins of kings, queens, and the wealthiest chieftains. Some of these longships have been discovered in such remarkable condition that even the vegetable matter buried with the dead has survived. Vikings considered the longship to be one of the most valuable possessions they owned, and they presumed the departed would spend eternity on some heavenly sea, continuing the adventures they had enjoyed during their earthly life.

The fronts of Viking ships were often carved into the likeness of a dragon's head to ward off the ferocious beasts and evil spirits of the sea.

Every Viking's heart followed the sea, and the only way to master the sea was the longship. The longship was at the core of Viking culture. No matter what the people might do when they were on land, the sea always called them back. Even farmers and colonists spent a great deal of time at sea. During this time, the longship was their fortress, their conveyance, their home.

A SEAFARING PEOPLE

"From the wrath of the Northmen, O Lord, deliver us!"[2] According to historian Gerald Simons, this prayer was often heard throughout western Europe between A.D. 800 and 1100. The Northmen were a group of people also known as Vikings, and they were fierce warriors in search of riches and slaves.

The Vikings came from the northern countries of Norway, Denmark, and Sweden, known collectively as Scandinavia. They spoke the same language and had the same customs and lineage. The word *Viking* may come from the Scandinavian word *vik*, meaning "bay" or "creek." It "may have originally referred to raiders who lurked in inlets and bays, waiting to strike,"[3] writes scholar Frank R. Donovan. In time, a person who went to sea in search of adventure was said (in the Viking's language) to go *i-viking*.

Since the growing season was so short in Scandinavia, Vikings took to the sea in search of spoils elsewhere.

WHY LONGSHIPS WERE SO IMPORTANT TO THE VIKINGS

While people of other lands relied on horses or oxen for transportation, the terrain of Scandinavia made such travel difficult. Gerald Simons eloquently describes the northland in *Barbarian Europe*.

Since rough, craggy mountains made up much of their interior landscape and roads often turned into rivers of mud, the inhabitants of Scandinavia quite naturally took to the sea. Villages were usually built on or near the coast, where deep fjords offered sheltered harbors; along the west coast of Norway, a belt of thousands of islands also helped to break wild storms and offer calm sailing. Inevitably the Vikings' economy depended on boats, for fishing, for ferrying supplies of furs and food and for travel up and down the coast, as well as for more far-reaching voyages of exploration and trade.

The sea was always important to the Vikings because vast forests, high mountains, and deep fjords (which are long, narrow arms of the sea bordered on each side by high cliffs) made it difficult to travel inland. The early settlements had to be along the coast and wherever natural clearings made farming possible. Because the land was not very fertile, even farmers relied on the sea to supplement their food.

THE VIKING CLASS SYSTEM

These farmers were called *carls*, or peasants, and made up the large middle class. According to Bertil Almgren, a professor at Uppsala University in Sweden, "They were free and had the right to carry arms and to appear before the *thing* (local assembly) in their capacity as landowners."[4] The upper class was made up of the powerful chieftains, or earls, and above all others were the kings. The chieftains, like the kings, were chosen by the people. They were responsible for leading the raids and expeditions, but if they were unsuccessful or unfair to their people, another leader would be chosen.

Although the eldest son of the king was expected to become the ruler after the old king died, he could only rule if the people swore their loyalty to him. If they refused, another king would be chosen to take his place.

Craftsmen made up a small part of the *carl* class. While almost everything the family needed was produced on the farm, a few items required special skills. Skilled craftsmen included blacksmiths, carpenters, wood carvers, and boat builders. Luxury items, such as iron cauldrons, spearheads inlaid with copper and silver, or shears for cutting thin metal, had to be bought from merchants, who might also own farms.

The lowest class was called the thralls. The thralls did all of the manual labor in Viking society. As Almgren notes,

> To the thralls was assigned all the hard, unspecified work, which required nothing but physical strength. They virtually belonged to their masters from birth. They had no legal rights and, of course, were not allowed to carry arms.[5]

If a free woman had a baby by a thrall, she became a thrall, too. If a man had a baby with a thrall, however, he continued to be free. In most other ways, women and men were considered equals. Women were rulers of the house, and when their men were at sea, they were also in charge of the farmlands. Occasionally they also went *i-viking* with their husbands, brothers, or fathers.

WITHIN THE FAMILY

Children were of great importance. Sons and daughters were needed to help with the work, but the Vikings also treasured their children and considered them to be important members of the family. To a Viking, the family was important as a whole unit. Each person in it contributed to make up that family unit, and decisions were made for the good of the family rather than for the good of an individual. Since the family would die out without children, sons and daughters were vital links to the future.

Old people had little value in Viking society. The way of life in the north was harsh and everyone had to do their share of the work. When a person grew too old to do this, they became an obstacle to the family. If it became necessary to leave home in stormy or freezing weather, an old person went on the errand because they were not so important to the survival of the family. The loss of an elderly grandmother had less impact than the loss of a strong, healthy son or daughter.

The Vikings' view of the family as all-important may have resulted in overpopulation, which is thought to be one reason the Vikings started raiding their neighboring countries. Northmen families were large, partly because Vikings could have several wives at the same time. The native soil was so poor and the winters so harsh, however, that it was difficult to feed large families. Even successful hunters would have found it difficult to bring down enough game to feed everyone. As Donovan explains, "For individual families who began to feel the economic pinch, and particularly for younger brothers who would not inherit land, the only answer was to go *i viking*."[6]

Overpopulation, along with improvements in shipbuilding and navigation, probably gave this seafaring people all the incentive they needed for challenging the open sea.

EVEN THEIR DEATHS WERE CENTERED AROUND THE SEA

The sea was so much a part of their lives that when the great chieftains, kings, and queens died, they were often cremated with their boats.

Because the Vikings believed that after a person's death, he or she would need their possessions for the afterlife, personal belongings were buried with them. Favorite animals and sometimes

A GOOD HARVEST

With so little fertile land and such a short growing season, the Vikings were never certain if the spring crops would yield enough food to feed their families through the winter. To please their gods, who they believed controlled the growth of crops, they performed ceremonies each spring that were intended to bring forth a good harvest. Gerald Simons describes these ceremonies in *Barbarian Europe*.

Carts . . . were decked with garlands of flowers surrounding a wooden statue of the fertility god, Freyr. Drawn by a horse, the cart went from village to village, as hopeful farmers and their families welcomed it with flowers and sacrifices. If their prayers were answered there would be adequate, if not abundant, supplies of the staples of the Viking diet: wheat and barley, fruit, cabbages and onions, as well as pork and beef. Should crops fail, as sometimes happened, families would be reduced to eating lichen, seaweed and the bark of trees.

Vikings believed that they would need their belongings in the afterlife. When they died they were buried in their ships with all their valuable possessions.

a wife or thrall were killed and put on the boat with a chief. The dead man's favorite utensils and tools were also put on board. Because kings and queens were richer than men or women in the middle or lower classes, it was reasoned that they would require more belongings to accompany them into the afterlife.

When everything was in place, the longship was returned to the water. As it drifted out with the tide, torches were thrown onto it. Soon the boat and all it carried would catch fire and, as it burned, sink into the sea.

Other important people were buried on the land with their entire ship. Most of these burials were on high, open ground not too far from water. Because the hole would have to be dug deep, a hill provided more dirt; likewise, if there were no trees or tree roots on the hill, the hole would be easier to dig. A waterway was also necessary because the ship could be rowed as close as possible to the site but would then have to be carried the rest of the way.

When the burial site was selected, a large hole was dug in the clay, the ship was brought as far as possible by water, then it was dragged or carried the rest of the way and lowered into the hole. Natural properties of the clay kept most of the ship from rotting; as a result, archaeologists centuries later have been able to uncover the secrets of Viking burials. Only the tall prow with the carved dragon head or other decoration stuck out of the hole once the burial was finished, and only that part was destroyed by the weather.

In 1867 archaeologists at Oseberg, Norway, uncovered the burial site of a Viking queen who is thought to have lived in A.D. 800. Along with her buried ship, researchers also found cooking utensils, such as pots and pans, wooden ladles, and plates, as well as wooden buckets that once held food. Sledges (wooden wagons mounted on runners to glide over grass or snow) were ornately carved and decorated with black, brown, and red paint. Because she was a queen and was quite rich, she also had several wagons on her boat. At the time it was very difficult to make wheels, so only the most important people could afford to own a wagon.

People with less money and importance also wanted to be buried in ships, so a ceremony was created to please them. According to Almgren,

Most of what is known about the Vikings comes from what they left behind. This ship is one of the few that has remained intact after lying for centuries in the Scandinavian soil.

Instead of a real ship or boat, the cremation grave was surrounded by a ship-shaped ring of stones, the deceased being supposed to possess sufficient magic power to change the stone ship into a real one that could carry him to his destination.[7]

For the warrior, whether rich or poor, the destination for the dead was Valhalla, the Viking heaven.

THE VIKING HEAVEN

Reigning over Valhalla was the powerful god Odin. He is depicted as a god of battle, but he is also the god of poetry and magic. Warriors and princes followed Odin and expected to reside with him after death, where they would fight endless and glorious battles and where their wounds would be miraculously healed so they could continue to fight forever.

The second of the three principal gods was Thor, the sky and thunder god, who watched over farmers and sailors. His symbol was the hammer, and many Vikings wore a small hammer as a

One of the wheelbarrows found buried with a Viking queen in the Oseberg ship. Several of these ornately carved wagons were found along with many of her other possessions.

piece of jewelry. When a thrall died, it was believed that Thor would watch over him for eternity because thralls were not allowed to carry weapons and therefore they could not achieve a warrior's death and fight beside Odin.

Freya, Odin's wife, was a fertility goddess (sometimes referred to as Frigg or as Freyr or Frey in the male form) closely linked with the moon and its phases. Freya was the commander of the Valkyries, who hovered near battles to take the souls of slain warriors to Valhalla.

Because the Vikings believed a warrior was assured a place in Valhalla, they were not afraid of death in battle, but they had contempt for a man who died of illness or of old age in bed. This was called a "straw death" and was not honorable. This belief made them fierce in battle and unafraid of dying.

The Viking Culture

Whether the Vikings were noble adventurers or barbaric savages has been debated for generations. The peoples they attacked, no doubt, saw them as evil, while later generations who read of their exploits probably view them more as brave explorers and intrepid seamen.

All agree they were fierce. As Donovan writes,

This is a tapestry with representations of two Norse gods. Thor, god of thunder, is on the right and Odin, god of war, is on the left.

All the non-Viking sources present the Northmen as complete villains—cruel, ruthless, vicious, bloodthirsty—slaying, pillaging, and burning all in their path. . . . The [Viking] sagas, on the other hand, present the Vikings as brave heroes fighting against great odds. These accounts admit that the Northmen plundered. In fact, the sagas brag of it.[8]

Although they have been called barbarians, the Vikings had a distinct civilization and culture. They governed themselves

Many Vikings were not the full-time, bloodthirsty plunderers that most thought them to be. During most of the year many of them lived as peaceful farmers.

and had a system of law, and those who broke the laws were punished. The Vikings' lives were relatively peaceful for much of the year and not unlike those whom they raided. Donovan describes their lifestyle: "When they were not out *i viking,* many of them were peaceful farmers. Most of the early raids were made in the spring, after the planting, and in the fall, after the harvest."[9]

Over the years, more and more Vikings began to spend the winters in the European countries rather than return home to Scandinavia after the raids. Those who stayed often married into local families and adopted the ways of the local culture.

Although they had a written language, the Vikings had no paper, and stone was too difficult to cut for detailed histories to be written. Therefore, much of what is known about the Vikings comes from stories written by the people in the lands they conquered or from Viking stories told and retold and written down much later.

PREPARING THE LONGSHIPS FOR SPRING RAIDS

From these stories, historians have pieced together a picture of Viking life at home and at sea. They know, for example, that during the long Scandinavian winter the longships were put in boat sheds to protect them from the freezing water that could crack their wooden hulls. As the rivers and fjords thawed, the longships were brought out of storage. As author John Mills writes,

> Using lengths of pine trunks as rollers they would push their ships down to the edge of the water and set them afloat once more. All along the coastline of Norway, in every fjord, the same scene would be taking place, as the coming of spring awoke the tribes.

The dragon-heads at the prows of the longboats would be repainted in bright colours, and new masts would be cut and shaped to replace those from the last season of raiding, which might have been damaged or weakened by the fierce winds encountered in constant sailing.[10]

In Scandinavia the nights are long in winter and little can be done outside. The women used this time to weave the sails that the longships would need in the spring. They wove long strips of heavy cloth in different colors so the boats could be identified from a distance at sea. The sight of these brightly colored sails would terrify the people who lived along the coasts and up the rivers of England, Brittany, Ireland, and other points in Europe when the Vikings arrived to plunder the countryside.

CALLING THE MEN TO EMBARK ON THE RAID

When the longships were ready in early May, the jarl, who was the leader of the village, blew on a large horn signaling that another season's raids were ready to begin. When the Vikings heard the awaited sound, they boarded their ships. As they left the village and floated down the rivers and fjords to the sea, they sang war songs.

When Vikings set out to sea, they often expected to be gone for long periods of time. If their aim was to explore or to set up trade routes, they might be gone an entire year or even longer. Those who left their homeland because of trouble with the law or the desire to find new, more fertile land to claim as their own sometimes took their families with them. According to Mills, "The bigger longboats would often be towing smaller boats which carried the wives and children, together with provisions and weapons."[11]

Most Viking raids took place in the spring and fall, before and after the growing season. The village leader blew on a horn to signal the men that a raid was to begin.

Though many Viking raids were conducted by small groups, they sometimes banded to-gether to form a large fleet to attack a city. Many Vikings remained in the territories they plundered and adopted local customs.

The longships were made to cross vast stretches of ocean, but their success was due to the Vikings themselves. They were free men bent on discovery and on gaining wealth. Their desire for adventure and wealth was aided by a knowledge of navigation and sailing that enabled them to cross uncharted distances far from landmarks of any kind.

Shipbuilding and Navigation

The inhabitants of Scandinavia had been building light, flexible vessels long before the Viking era began. These vessels enabled them to navigate through the fjords, rivers, and seas of their native land. Viking shipbuilders added to that legacy by modifying the size and shape of the hull and the methods used to construct it. They also expanded their ability to control the ship's direction with improvements in the keel, and they added a sail that allowed them to voyage far beyond their own coastline. These and other improvements made it possible for the Vikings to cross deep and sometimes stormy oceans, to maneuver through shallow water and narrow passages, to carry crew and cargo, and to sail in a swift and sure manner to destinations around the globe.

The Early Ships

One of the earliest Scandinavian ships was discovered in Als in southwest Denmark and is called the Hjortspring ship. This was the first known ship to overlap the planks along the sides in the manner later used in the longships. The ship was probably built around 300 B.C. and was probably used as a war canoe before being sunk in a lake along with the weapons of several warriors (probably as a sacrifice) in about 350 B.C.

Bertil Almgren describes the boat as being

> about fifty feet long and formed of five broad, thin slightly overlapping boards which were stitched together with hide thongs. The boards and the gunwales were not joined at the stem [front end of the boat] and stern [rear end of the boat] but were run into hollowed-out end-pieces fixed to the bottom plank fore [front] and aft [behind].[12]

This method of attaching the boards and gunwales was later used in the longships and allowed the flexibility necessary for ocean voyages.

The boards were cut to make wedge-shaped pieces, or cleats, on the inside where hazel-wood ribs were fastened. These ribs were braced in place by the rower's seat, or thwart. The boat was propelled by paddles. This placement of the cleats, the distance between the ribs, and the use of thwarts would appear later in the longships.

More improvements were evident in the next stage of shipbuilding, not only in the size but also in the way the boards were fastened together and how the ship was propelled through the water. This ship is called the Nydam ship and was discovered on the Flensburger Fjord in southwest Denmark, where it was sunk, probably as a sacrificial offering similar to that of the Hjortspring ship.

This ship was probably made early in the fourth century A.D. and is much larger than the Hjortspring boat, measuring seventy-five feet in length. Each plank is long enough to run the entire length of the hull, which is the main body of the ship. The planks are held together by iron rivets, as would be used later in the longships. In the Nydam ship, the curved prow (which is the pointed and projecting front part) shows the distinctive profile of the longships beginning to evolve.

Like the Hjortspring ship, the oak ribs on the Nydam ship are tied to cleats. Oars, rather than paddles, propelled the ship and were probably held in place by bent branches secured to the rail. These were the forerunners of the oarlocks, which were necessary for greater speed and ease of rowing on the sea. The Nydam ship had no sail. Because the bottom planks were not strong enough to hold together in rough seas, the ship was built narrow, with a high bow. This narrow shape would later give the longships their speed in the water, and the high bow eventually would be carved with the feared dragon visage.

The next improvement in Scandinavian shipbuilding was discovered at Sunnmore in Norway and is known as the Kvalsund ship. This ship is about sixty-one feet long but is broader and more stable than the Nydam ship. A long spine beneath the ship provides the first indication of what would later become a keel. A keel strengthened the hull structure and gave its crew greater ability to control the ship's direction. Without the keel, the longships would not have been able to maintain a course in windy or stormy weather.

In the Kvalsund ship, the oars are held in place with oarlocks, which are fastened to the rails by wooden pegs called tre-

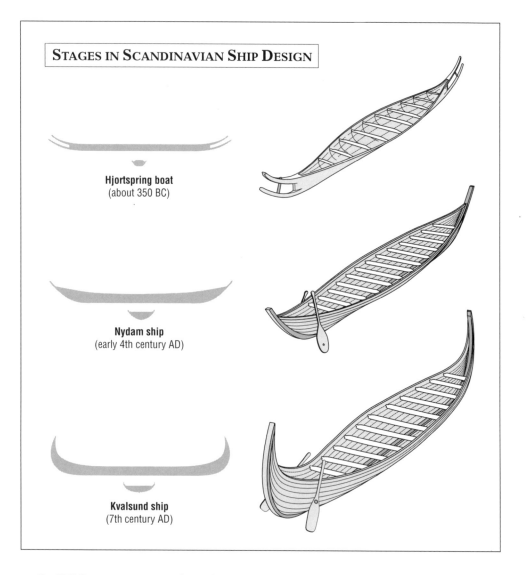

STAGES IN SCANDINAVIAN SHIP DESIGN

Hjortspring boat
(about 350 BC)

Nydam ship
(early 4th century AD)

Kvalsund ship
(7th century AD)

nails. While no mast was found, picture stones found in the Gotland region of Scandinavia suggest that sails were used beginning in the seventh century, placing the Kvalsund ship in that period. The sail would become part of the distinctive silhouette of the longship and an emblem easily recognizable while at sea.

The earliest Scandinavian sailing ship yet discovered was found in 1903 in a burial mound at Oseberg, west of Oslo fjord, and was built in about A.D. 820. In many ways, the Oseberg ship was the first true longship.

The Oseberg ship in the site where it was discovered. It is the earliest example of a Viking sailing ship that has ever been found.

The Oseberg ship has many features that would be built into the longships, such as a mast and a mast partner to hold it upright. Without the mast and strong bracing to hold the sail, ocean voyages and the speed necessary for raids would have been impossible. The distance between the ship's ribs was now a standard width, and the ribs were stronger because of the Oseberg innovations. Oarlocks were replaced by oarports so the hull could be built higher.

On the Oseberg ship, the mast is mounted on a keelson located just forward of the middle of the ship and is held in place by a mast partner called a *kloften,* so named because it is shaped like a fork. As one historian of the Viking period observes, "The mast partner had two functions, to guide the mast when it was raised and lowered, and to support it when the ship was under sail. It was, however, no substitute for shrouds, the ropes that supported the mast laterally."[13]

From the early Hjortspring ship to the end of the Viking period, the distance between the ship's ribs remained the same. They were located a little over three feet apart because that was the best possible distance between oarsmen, who were seated on thwarts.

In the ships built before the Oseberg, the ribs reach from gunwale to gunwale, regardless of how they were fastened to the hull. This made the hulls rounded in the middle and narrowed to a V-shape on either end. Hulls of that shape had poor lateral stability but were very fast. The Oseberg ship has greater stability because the ribs were made of several pieces of wood fastened together instead of single pieces of wood. A strake (a line of planks joined endwise from stem to stern) called a *meginhufr* spread the strain caused by the tops of the floor timbers.

By the time the Oseberg ship was built, improvements had also been made in the way the ship was rowed. Historian Peter Sawyer indicates some of the innovations:

> Instead of rowlocks on the gunwale the oars passed through oarports that could be closed when under sail. This enabled the oars to reach the water at a suitable angle, despite the greater size of the ship and its higher freeboard. The Oseberg ship, launched early in the ninth century, thus displays all the key features that distinguished Viking ships for the next 200 years.[14]

The innovations in Viking shipbuilding in the ninth century allowed the longships to travel great distances on the open ocean with a great deal of speed.

THE LONGSHIP IS DEVELOPED

The true longship was being built by the middle of the ninth century. It was a long, graceful wooden ship with a high, curving stem and stern. Carved into its stern were fierce dragon heads or decorative spirals. There was a square mast located near the middle of the ship that could be raised or lowered as the need arose. When not under sail, the ship could be rowed by men using oars fitted into oarlocks (with removable covers) located in the side of the hull.

The sides of the ship were fastened together in such a way as to allow the hull to flex with the waves, thus preventing it from breaking apart. The ship was large enough to carry cargo and passengers on long voyages, yet swift enough in the water to outdistance any other ship of its day. In this way, it served its masters well; it could be used as a warship or cargo vessel, or both—depending on the needs of the moment.

OBTAINING WOOD FOR THE LONGSHIPS

The longships were made of wood, and the planks had to be properly cut to give the most strength. Vikings made planks by splitting huge tree trunks, preferably oaks, which grew abundantly in southern Scandinavia. The trunks were split radially

The longships used by the Vikings were very versatile. They could be powered by sail or by oar, and they could function as warships or cargo vessels.

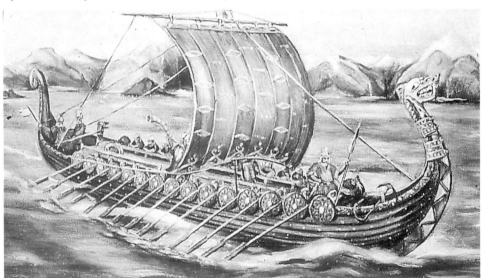

from large trees with as few knots as could be found. The planks were exceptionally strong because they followed the grain of the wood. Another advantage is that planks cut in this fashion shrink and warp very little as they dry. The builders also used freshly cut trees, which was very important since the new wood was easier to work than seasoned timber. Completed stem and stern posts were often stored under water to prevent them from cracking and warping later.

In northern Scandinavia the forests were mostly pine. Pines were split in two and each half was made into a wide plank. This method could also be used on oak and other trees when a particularly wide plank was needed.

The curved pieces, or those that required an angle, were usually made from wood that had naturally grown in that shape. This way the piece could be made from a single piece of wood, which cut down on the weight of the ship. As Sawyer notes,

> One of the main aims of Viking shipwrights was to make the construction light, flexible, and strong. The floor timbers were often shaped to be narrow and deep over the keel but flat and broad at their upper ends where the demand for flexibility was greatest.[15]

HOW THE SHIPS WERE BUILT

Shipbuilders knew exactly what the ship would look like before they started building, even though they had no written diagrams. The shape of the stem was based on segments of circles of varying sizes. The sizes of these arcs were determined by the length of the keel. The shipwright must have used some basic measure, perhaps a string with a bit of chalk on the end, to make the circles the correct sizes.

The ships were built from the bottom up rather than framing the entire ship and then going back over it to complete various parts. First, the keel and stems were made. As the strakes reached the proper heights, the interior was built. The frames were made as the bottom was completed; when the sides were high enough, cross beams were added.

The longships were made of wood, but the rivets that held them together were of iron. Viking ships had about five rivets in each yard of plank. Rivets were not difficult for the shipbuilders to make, but fashioning the large iron anchors required the expertise of a blacksmith.

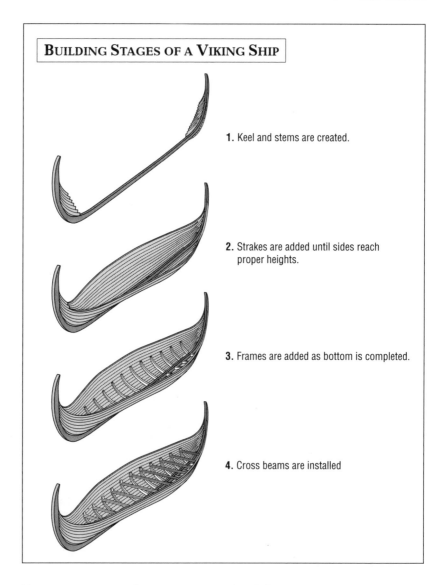

BUILDING STAGES OF A VIKING SHIP

1. Keel and stems are created.

2. Strakes are added until sides reach proper heights.

3. Frames are added as bottom is completed.

4. Cross beams are installed

IMPROVEMENTS CONTINUED TO BE MADE

Although ships of all sizes continued to be made during the Viking era, the seagoing ships had to be made stronger, larger, and faster as the voyages became longer and trading more important. Almgren explains how this was done:

> The ship sides were increased in height, so that what was formerly the thick, reinforced rail or gunwale timber, appeared far down along the side of the hull. The extra

planking above the waterline was fastened by wooden nails to naturally-bent branches called knees which were fixed to the cross beams. Probably the changes and additions to this and later craft were due to the fact that the ships carried mast and sail. The bottom was strengthened to carry the weight and stresses of the mast and the sides raised so that the vessel could heel without shipping water.[16]

THE IMPORTANCE OF THE SAIL

No matter how streamlined or seaworthy a ship might be, it required a great deal of muscle and exertion to row it on the open sea. To more easily travel the hundreds of miles between countries, a better device had to be found. The Vikings turned to the sail. Before the eighth century, Viking ships were built for rowing rather than for sea voyages or for sailing. Even with strong men working the oars, however, the ships could never have sped over the North Sea to raid countries hundreds of miles away. Once sails were added to ships, the sides were heightened and the hulls became longer and deeper, producing a ship that was graceful as well as swift.

The sail was held in place by a mast, or upright pole. The mast was held secure by a large block of wood called a *kjerringa,* which means "old woman" in Old Norse. The oak *kjerringa* was about as tall as a man and lay along the keel and across two ribs. Above the *kjerringa,* and also holding the mast erect, was a wooden object called a mastfish because of its shape. Without these innovations, the mast would topple over and cause injuries, be lost in the water, or even sink the ship.

When nearing land or navigating in shallow water, the sail was brought down and the ship was propelled by oars, which meant that there had to be a place for the oarsmen to sit. At first the men sat on the hull's cross beams to row. In the later longships, however, a removable deck was built over the crossbeams. As the ships were built longer, the sides were built higher and it

Before they made use of sails the Vikings' ships were powered entirely by oars. Sails allowed the Vikings to travel hundreds of miles across the seas.

became impractical to fasten the oars in oarlocks high along the top of the rail, so holes were cut in the sides of the hull. Oars, which were about eighteen feet long, were placed in the holes at the height suitable for a man to row when seated. Wooden covers concealed the holes when the sail was being used.

LONGSHIPS OFTEN USED WIND POWER

When at sea, the greatest speed could be reached by using the sail instead of the oars. No intact remains of a longship sail have been found, but drawings from that time period and eyewitness accounts describe a square sail, frequently colored in a distinctive way to make the ship recognizable at a distance.

The longship sail is believed to have measured 35½ to 40 feet wide. Because no complete mast has been found, no one knows how tall the sail might have stood. Evidence indicates that the sail was meant to be raised or lowered quickly and frequently on ropes made of hemp or of leather. This would signify that the sail and mast were of a size to be handled easily on the seas. If this assumption is correct, the sail and mast may have been smaller, and the longships may have been faster, than is usually assumed.

Wadmal, a rough woolen cloth used for the sail, was almost certainly woven by the women. Looms were simple and made of two upright boards that leaned against a wall. A horizontal board at the top held the warp, or threads, that hung down. These threads were

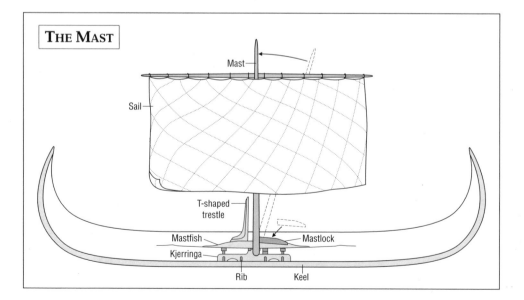

THE MAST

Mast

Sail

T-shaped trestle

Mastfish

Mastlock

Kjerringa

Rib

Keel

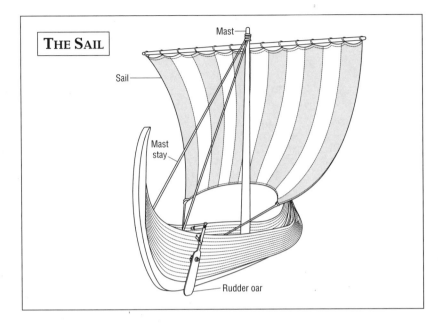

THE SAIL

Mast

Sail

Mast stay

Rudder oar

stretched tight by the means of warp weights made of stone or baked clay. Horizontal threads were passed through the warp, starting at the top and working downward. The finished pieces would be sewn together to make cloth large enough for the sail.

THE LONGSHIPS HAD TO BE WATERTIGHT

It was important to keep water out of the hull to prevent the ship from sinking, but the only way to row the ship was to cut holes in the sides. The largest Viking grave ship yet found is the Gokstad ship, discovered in 1880. There are sixteen oar holes in each side of the Gokstad ship, all cut in the fourteenth plank. To keep the sea out, wooden disks were hinged to the holes and could be shut from the inside when the oars were not being used. The rivets were hammered in from the outside into holes that had been drilled through the oak.

MAKING THE SHIPS MORE SEAWORTHY

As the voyages became longer, the ships had to be modified to sail through storms in high seas. The keel and cross beams were used to make the ship stronger beneath the waterline, where ocean waves would cause the most stress. Because the long-ships were wider than earlier boats, they were more stable in the water and less likely to tip over or bring in water.

A VIKING SHIPWRECK

Vikings had no fear of dying. Death at sea meant going to Valhalla to sail into battle with Odin, and every Viking wanted this. Even when facing certain death, the Vikings did not flinch. One of the early Northmen legends quoted by Bertil Almgren in *The Viking* is the *Saga of Torfinn Karlsvne*, which describes a Viking shipwreck.

Because of the tempest, Bjarne Grimoifson drifted with his ship to the Irish Sea, and they met a breaker, and the ship began to go down. They had a small boat greased with tar which protects against the seaworms. They entered the boat but realized that it could not carry all of them. Then said Bjarne, "Whereas the boat cannot carry more than half of our men, it is my advice that lots should be cast to settle who shall go into the boat, because this cannot be settled by rank." They all thought this very fair, so nobody objected. So they drew lots, and it fell to Bjarne's share to go in the boat with half of the men, because the boat could not carry any more.

A strong hull was of primary importance in stormy seas. Naval authority Guy R. Williams describes how a clinker-built hull, such as the Vikings used, was held together:

In a "clinker-built" hull, the planks are positioned so that they over-lap, and are held in place by being fastened on to underlying ribs and to each other. All clinker-built hulls can be recognized immediately by the ridges or steps that are produced where the exposed narrow sides of the planks meet, squarely, the broader surfaces of the planks that are placed next to them.[17]

HOW THE SHIP'S PLANKING WAS HELD TOGETHER

Since the Gokstad ship was found in good condition, historians and engineers have been able to determine how this clinker-built ship was constructed. To withstand a storm, the ship's planks had to be fastened together in such a way as to be strong but not so inflexible as to break apart.

On the Gokstad ship nearly all of the planks below the water-line are held together with strips of spruce root and are fastened to the ribs instead of to the keel. The board at the waterline, which in the earlier ships was the rail or gunwale, is the tenth plank up from the keel and is called *megin-hufr* in Old Norse. The board beneath that is not tied to the ribs but is held in place by trenails, as is the *meginhufr*. The boards above the waterline are fastened with trenails to wooden braces on the cross beams. These braces reach to the fourteenth board.

Because the planks were tied together rather than fastened more securely, the ship could twist about six inches from its original shape as it met strong waves and thus kept the ship from being torn to pieces in storms.

This is the reconstructed Gokstad ship. It is the largest Viking grave ship ever found.

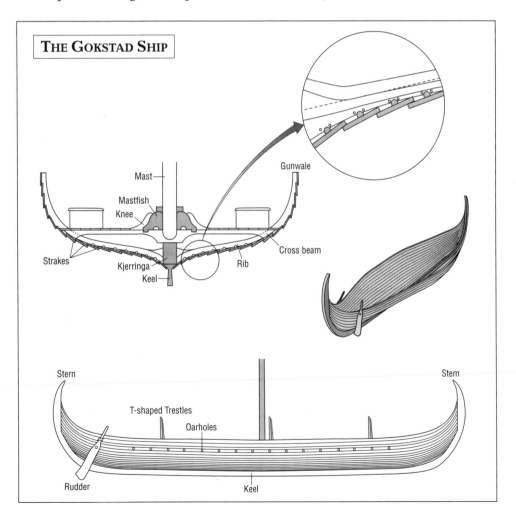

THE GOKSTAD SHIP

Mast

Mastfish

Knee

Gunwale

Strakes

Kjerringa

Keel

Rib

Cross beam

Stern

T-shaped Trestles

Oarholes

Stem

Rudder

Keel

THE DRAGON SHIPS

The longships were sleek and beautiful. They were built to slip through the water with little resistance and must have sailed gracefully. According to naval historian Frank O. Braynard,

> The ship was their instrument of conquest. Despite their ferocious nature, they had poetry in their hearts, as the names of their sleek double-ended long ships show. There was a *Lion of the Waves*, a *Horse of the Gull's Trace*, and a *Reindeer of the Breeze*.[18]

Not every Viking expedition ended in conquest. Some Vikings were eager to explore new lands and set up new trade routes.

Dominating the prow of the longships were carvings of fear-some beasts, frequently a dragon or sea serpent.

Not all the Northmen went *i-viking*. Some were more inter-ested in setting up trade routes or in exploring. Although the cargo ships might have been a bit larger and less swift than the warships, the design was that of a longship.

It was believed in those days that terrible monsters lurked in the oceans, and many ships sunk by storms were believed to have been attacked by sea serpents. To protect the ship and crew against these monsters, the prows were carved to repre-sent fearsome beasts wicked enough to frighten the sea ser-pents. As Gerald Simons writes,

> After the crops were in the ground and the days grew long and clear enough for sailing, Viking seamen left their families to embark on voyages that might take them to the very edge of the world, where mists ob-scured vision and ships sometimes mysteriously disap-peared. To frighten off foes and evil spirits of the ocean, these mariners sailed under awesome figureheads . . . which, combined with their vessels' long, serpentine sil-houettes, led to the name "dragon ships."[19]

HOW THE VIKINGS NAVIGATED THEIR SHIPS

Always in the Vikings' life was the sea. While wives and chil-dren often went with the men on expeditions, navigation was the specialty of the men. Just as girls were taught to cook and run a household, boys were taught from early childhood how to judge the speed and direction of the wind and when to expect the tides to rise and fall.

As long as land was in sight, it was easy to find one's way and seafaring people from many countries knew how to do this. However, no one knows exactly how the Vikings were able to navigate once they were out of sight of land.

The Vikings most certainly steered by noting where the stars were in the sky as well as where the sun rose and set. This is called celestial navigation, and it is the oldest means of finding directions. A good ship's captain was said to have a "sixth sense" to tell him how to cross uncharted seas and the Atlantic Ocean.

Historians believe the Vikings may have had a primitive as-trolabe, an instrument that was held in the hand and pointed at certain stars to tell which way the boat was traveling. So far, no astrolabe has been found in a Viking ship, but experts say such accurate navigation would have been almost impossible without something of this kind.

NAVIGATING WITH THE HELP OF BIRDS

One method probably used for finding land beyond the horizon was to watch the birds flying overhead. As evening approaches, most birds find land to roost for the night. By watching which way gannets and other birds flew as the sun was setting, the navigator knew which direction to turn the ship and could follow the birds to land.

An Irish legend says Vikings carried cages of crows with them on their ships. If they lost sight of land, a seaman would set a crow free. The crow would instinctively head for land, and the Vikings would steer the longship in the direction the crow flew. According to the legend, the crows could find land even from far out at sea. This legend may have been the basis for the expression, "Straight as the crow flies."

NAVIGATING BY THE STARS AND SUN

At night the Vikings used the stars to chart their courses. The North Star has always been a reliable guidepost for sailors. During the summer months, however, when nighttime is no darker than twilight, the stars were too pale to use as guides. During these months of endless days, the navigator used the sun.

Over the years men watched to see exactly where the sun would rise and set every day, and a seasoned navigator could reckon his location by using his stored knowledge. A method was needed, however, to enable less experienced Vikings to travel from one place to another. A Viking from Iceland named Stjerne-Oddi compiled a chart showing the sun's altitude for an entire year as well as a table showing the direction of dawn and twilight. By using this chart, navigators less educated in how to sail a longship from one place to another could find their way with ease.

Almgren explains the Viking method of calculating the direction a longship was sailing:

> All the measurements of angles were made in what was called a "half wheel," a kind of half sun-diameter, which corresponds to about sixteen seconds of an arc. This was something which was known to every skipper at that time, or by the "long-voyage pilot" or *kendtmand* (man

In order to find their way at sea, Vikings used the sun, the stars, and sometimes birds to navigate their ships.

who knows) who sometimes went along on voyages when the skipper was himself unfamiliar with the route. When the sun was in the sky, it was not, therefore, difficult to find the four points of the compass, and the determining of latitude did not cause any problems either. [20]

The latitude could be determined by the altitude of the sun, and to do so, an instrument called a *solbradt,* or "sun-board," was used. The *solbradt* was divided into "half wheels" that could be used for an accurate measure of latitude. Although a *solbradt* is mentioned in Norse legends, one has yet to be found.

In sunny weather, it was possible to steer a straight course along a latitude. Almgren writes that "the course could be regulated every noon by means of the 'sun-board.' If the angle to the sun was larger, the ship had drifted southwards; if it was smaller, the course had slipped too far north." [21]

FINDING THEIR WAY WHEN LOST

During storms the shipmaster had to concentrate on keeping the ship from sinking. After the storm passed and the weather cleared, he would try to figure out where the ship had been carried by the wind and waves.

TOOLS USED BY THE SHIPBUILDERS

Trees to be used for planks were cut down with long-handled axes with narrow blades. The trunks were split by hammering wedges into the wood grain. Once the planks were cut, they were shaped with smaller axes with broad blades, which were also used in battle and can be seen on the Bayeux Tapestry. The planks were probably made where the tree was cut down since there would be no reason to haul the entire trunk to the ship-building site.

Although the Vikings had planes to smooth the wood, they instead smoothed the planks with their hand axes. The planes were used to trim the overlapping edges to make a close fit. A groove was cut with a tool called a mould scraper and was stuffed with wool yarn to make the joint watertight. The mould scraper was also used to make designs in the wood for decorative purposes. To make a hole, the Vikings used a spoon-shaped bore that was twisted into the wood while pressure was placed on a breastplate. No one knows what measuring instruments were used, but the Vikings were certain to have had plumb lines as well as staves and strings divided into some standard measure.

It was more difficult to determine how far the ship had traveled. An experienced seaman could guess at speed by the size of the bow-wave and how the ship heeled in relation to the wind. Experts believe maps and estimations of distance were memorized and were as reliable to the Vikings as any map or chart drawn on paper.

THE SUN-STONE

No one knows if the Vikings had compasses, but more than one saga mentions an object called a sun-stone. This object was probably used to navigate in much the same way a compass can be used to find true north.

In one of the sagas, a Viking king called the Holy King Olaf and his navigator, Sigurd Syr, become lost during a winter storm. An excerpt from the saga records that it was foggy and it was snowing heavily. The king asked a man to take a look outside and the sky was cloud-covered. He then asked Sigurd to tell him where the sun could be and he [Sigurd] told him. Then the king picked up the "sun-stone" and he then saw how the stone was radiating and out of that he made the conclusion that Sigurd was right.[22]

Early compasses were probably small magnetic stones floating on a piece of wood in water. With this, Sigurd would have been able to tell where the sun was if he knew the hour of the day. Magnetic stones, however, do not radiate. No sun-stone has been found, and it is uncertain why a stone would appear to give off light. This strange behavior of the stone may have been an embellishment added by the storyteller of the saga for dramatic effect.

Considering the Vikings had no written records to chart oceans or paper to draw ship plans, they accomplished an amazing feat in creating the longships and sailing them so far from home. It was a feat they accomplished over and over again. In historian Frank R. Donovan's opinion, "Viking ships were the fastest things afloat in their day, and for many years after. They were the most seaworthy vessels of the age, the only vessels that could safely cope with the perils of the open sea."[23]

LIFE AT SEA

Long before the fjords thawed in the spring and the longships were taken from winter storage, the Vikings prepared for voyages. The ships were examined for wear and damage, any leaks were repaired, ropes made of animal skin or plant fiber were mended or replaced with new ones, and the sail was examined for tears and worn spots.

The entire family was involved in the preparations. Men repaired the ships, sharpened the weapons, replaced ax handles, and did the chores needing the most muscle. Women finished weaving the sails and sewing them together to catch the wind, and they mended the clothing that would be taken on the voyage. Children helped their parents and, in doing so, learned what they would need to know as adults when they would prepare for voyages of their own. Children who were not needed to help in preparations, as well as the elderly, looked after the younger children and babies. Young and old women saw to the preparation and storing of food that would be needed on the voyage.

MAKING SALTED MEAT AND FISH

Domestic animals were killed in the winter to use as food on the spring voyages. The cold temperature helped protect the meat until it was cured, or preserved. Once the meat had been cut off the carcass, it was salted or smoked so it would not spoil on the long voyages. This method of preserving meat has changed little over the centuries. For people living near the sea, salt was plentiful. It was obtained simply by boiling sea water until the liquid was gone and the salt remained.

After the raw meat had been cut into smaller pieces, it was placed in a box on a bed of salt. More salt was poured on top of it, and another piece of meat could then be added as well as more salt. It was important that all the meat be completely covered by the salt. If the family wanted to eat some of the meat, they would slice off the amount needed, wash away the salt, soak it overnight, then cook it the next day.

SMOKING MEAT TO PRESERVE IT

Meat would have been smoked either immediately after killing and butchering the animal or in the spring when the warmer temperatures started thawing the salted meat. In America, the method for smoking meat is to use a small building called a smokehouse. The Vikings must have used a similar structure since it is important to surround the meat with heat and smoke for a period of time. Holes would have been poked in the meat and wooden rods run through them. The rods could be hung on pegs or joists in the smokehouse.

The Foxfire Book, compiled by a teacher named Eliot Wigginton, describes life in the Appalachian region of America and tells how meat is smoked. The methods the Vikings used were probably similar.

> A fire was built inside the [smoke] house. If it had a dirt floor, the fire could be built right on the floor. Otherwise, a wash pot was set in the middle of the room and a fire built in that. The fire itself was made of small green chips of hickory or oak. . . . Using this fuel, the smoke was kept billowing through the house for from two to six days, or until the meat took on the brown crust that was desired both for its flavor, and for its ability to keep flies and insects out of the meat.[24]

WHAT THEY MAY HAVE EATEN AND DRUNK ON VOYAGES

No one is certain what the Vikings ate on the long voyages. No cooking fire could have been built on shipboard, so their food must have been preserved by salting or smoking before they left home or was eaten raw. Historian Bertil Almgren describes their probable diet:

> Dried and salted fish or meat with water, and sour milk or beer to drink must have been their staple diet. In both the Oseberg and Gokstad ships large cauldrons, perhaps for cooking on shore, were found. At Oseberg, in addition to cauldrons, a real piece of camping equipment turned up, a collapsible iron tripod for hanging the pots over a fire.[25]

The cauldrons were large enough to cook soup or broth for everyone on the ship.

Large supplies of water would have been necessary, especially on voyages where they would travel for long stretches without sighting land. The water was probably stored in large skin bags. Before sailing, the water bags and other necessities were carried onto the ship and stowed carefully to take up the least amount of room. These preparations would have been as familiar to the Vikings as the chores performed in their homes on land.

THE VIKINGS' SECOND HOME

The Vikings might be said to have two homes, one on land and one at sea. They thought nothing of embarking on voyages that would take weeks or months. If they sailed late in the year, they frequently planned not to return to Scandinavia until the following spring or even later.

When Viking women and children accompanied the men on long voyages, there seems to have been little in the way of special provisions. Privacy must have been almost unknown, as the

The Vikings spent so much time at sea (sometimes more than a year) that it was referred to as their second home. On long voyages wives and children were sometimes brought along.

THERE WERE GREAT PERILS AT SEA

Pirates and storms were not the only perils at sea. Occasionally huge whirlpools could swallow a longship, crew and all, with almost no warning. In A.D. 1076, historian Adam of Bremen described a terrible whirlpool in the waters off Greenland in the North Atlantic during the eighth century. In *The Viking*, Bertil Almgren records Adam's account of the dangerous adventure.

> Of a sudden they fell into that numbing ocean's dark mist which could hardly be penetrated with the eyes. And, behold, the current of the fluctuating ocean whirled back to its mysterious fountainhead and with most furious impetuosity drew the unhappy sailors, who in their despair now thought only of death, on to chaos; this they say is the abysmal chasm—that deep in which, reports has it, all the back flow of the sea, which appears to decrease, is absorbed and in turn revomited, as the mounting fluctuation is usually described. As the partners were imploring the mercy of God to receive their souls, the backward thrust of the sea carried away some of their ships, but its forward ejection threw the rest far behind the others. Freed thus by the timely help of God from the instant peril they had before their eyes, they seconded the flood by rowing with all their might.

ships had no separate cabins. At the most, a cloth screen might have been hung to block the sight of those on board. The chores of the women and children at sea probably included fishing, which would have freed the men for rowing and more strenuous jobs.

How They Fished

Although fish was a big part of the Vikings' diet, especially when they were at sea, few examples of nets, hooks, or fish traps have been found. Despite the absence of such implements, historians believe the Vikings were skilled at harvesting the sea's bounty. As Almgren writes,

A specialized form of hunting was the pursuit of the big sea-mammals such as whales, seals and walruses. The walrus was particularly sought after. Almost every part of it could be used: the teeth were valuable as a substitute for ivory, [which was used in decorations, inlays, and jewelry as well as for trading] the meat was eatable, and the best ship-ropes were made of strips of walrus skin.[26]

No evidence has been found to indicate that Vikings used harpoons to hunt whales. It is believed that they may have herded the giant mammals into shallow creeks where they could be killed more easily than in deep water.

ENTERTAINMENT AT SEA

When not fishing or doing other chores, both young and old Vikings must have needed ways to pass the time. A number of whistles and games have been found in the burial ships, and the

Vikings must have taken such pastimes with them to amuse themselves while at sea. According to historian Tony D. Triggs, "They played all sorts of musical instruments, including whistles made from sticks or birds' bones. They also liked board games."[27] Chess was a popular game, and they carved chess pieces out of walrus tusks or bone. Backgammon was also well liked.

During the long voyages, time was almost certainly passed by telling stories. Each generation of Vikings learned about their predecessors by the legends passed on by word of mouth. Because the Vikings were accustomed to hearing and repeating stories, they would have had many tales to draw on. This fascination for repeating legends accounts for the popularity of skalds, wandering bards or storytellers, in the Viking community.

To pass the time on long sea voyages the Vikings played many varieties of games. This piece is a king from a chess set.

The skalds were very popular with people who had little entertainment, and they were probably welcomed aboard the ships. When there was no skald aboard, the storytelling probably fell to one of the elders, a person who had spent the most years listening to and learning stories.

Storytellers, or skalds, were very popular in Viking communities. The skalds would tell stories about the creation of Earth and the Norse gods to pass the long winter nights.

STORIES TOLD BY THE SKALDS

The nights on the voyage would have been passed hearing ancient myths, such as the story of how the earth was created. The Vikings believed the world was a circular island inhabited by Midgard, who were a tribe of men. The island was supposed to have been made from the body of a giant named Ymer, who was killed by his grandsons Odin, Ve, and Vili.

They also believed that one day their gods would be involved in a great battle against Fire Giants from a country called Muspell. As historian John Geipel records, "Odin would be devoured by a monstrous wolf, Thor fatally bitten by the venomous serpent called Jormungand, and Frey stabbed to death by the giant chieftain, Surt. The catastrophe would end with Surt setting fire to the world."[28]

One of the favorite sagas, *Havamal*, tells about the creation of the Viking alphabet. According to the saga, Odin discovers runes after hanging himself as a sacrifice in a tree for nine nights (as was customary for the Vikings to hang their animal sacrifices). The runes were a sixteen-letter alphabet of twiglike figures. Vikings often carved runes on stones wherever they landed or to commemorate a great person or brave deed. The story of Odin's ordeal in discovering them must have held the listeners enthralled.

POPULAR STORIES OF FAMOUS VIKINGS

They also enjoyed stories of brave men such as Toki Gormsson, a Danish chieftain. At the Battle of Fyrisvall near Uppsala, Toki burned his ships to force his men and himself to fight to the death.

Women also figured in the tales. One such tale involved a beautiful, wise, and clever queen named Thyri, wife of King Gorm. In her effort to protect Denmark from the Swedes and Germans, Thyri recruited men to build a protective barrier on the country's southern border. She also resisted the efforts of the German emperor who wanted to steal her away from her husband.

The Norse god of war, Odin, is credited with discovering the runes. The runes are the sixteen-letter Viking alphabet.

While living on shipboard must have had its boring hours, there were also times of excitement and fear, for the ocean was still uncharted and terrible beasts were rumored to live there. Aside from mythical beasts, there was the possibility of discovering new and strange lands.

BOARDING AND LEAVING THE SHIP

Once they reached land, gangplanks were used by the Vikings to board and leave the ships and by animals being brought on board. These were made from long, narrow boards with steps cut into them.

When the destinations were reached and it was time to unload the animals, the ships were drawn in as close to land as possible and maneuvered so that the side of the ship paralleled the shore. The animals then were driven over the side of the ship and into the shallow water. The weight of animals crowding to one side would have lowered that side so it would have been easy for them to jump over. The Vikings' horses were a smaller breed than is common now, and they would have fit more comfortably on the longships.

HOW THE LONGSHIPS WERE ROWED

The longships did not always rely on their sail. When the wind was strong and steady or the ship needed more accurate handling, such as when preparing for battle or for docking, the ships were rowed. In many of the longships that have been excavated, there were no fixed benches. The crew sat on their sea chests to row, which not only saved the shipbuilder from making benches but also made use of chests that would otherwise have merely sat about taking up precious space. For this reason, the sea chests were all made the same size, which was the perfect height for a man to sit upon and row.

The large longships had holes for the oars to fit into, but the smaller ones used a board with natural crooks or bends in it to act as an oarlock. A loop of rope kept the oars in place while they were being used. While most of the oars were probably plain and unadorned, the ones found on the Oseberg ship had a tongue groove on the blade and decorative moldings along the edges.

When preparing for battle or sailing in close quarters, the Vikings relied on their oars for precision maneuvering.

Animals were not taken on all voyages. If the Vikings were on a raid and not intending to build a settlement, they took no horses. Once they reached land, they stole whatever horses they needed.

A VIKING CAMP

Whenever possible the Vikings moored their ships near land in the evenings. According to the sagas, they preferred sleeping on land to sleeping on the ship. They erected cloth tents that were held up by lightweight wooden frames. Although none of the cloth coverings have survived the centuries, the wooden supports have. One was found in the Gokstad ship and two more in the Oseberg ship. One of the tent frames was decorated with paintings of serpents, a magical symbol probably meant to frighten away evil spirits and to protect the sleepers during the night.

BEOWULF'S LONGSHIP

The oldest known story written in Old English was a saga from the eighth century about a Viking hero named Beowulf. Beowulf kills the monster Grendel and Grendel's fearsome mother. In the end, Beowulf defeats a dragon but dies from his wounds. In *Barbarian Europe,* Gerald Simons records how the Viking longship is described with great pride.

> He gave command for a goodly vessel
> Fitted and furnished . . .
> Came the hour of boarding; the boat was riding
> The waves of the harbor under the hill.
> The eager mariners mounted the prow;
> Billows were breaking, sea against sand.
> In the ship's hold snugly they stowed their trappings,
> Gleaming armor and battle-gear;
> Launched the vessel, the well-braced bark,
> Seaward bound on a joyous journey.
> Over breaking billows, with bellying sail
> And foamy beak, like a flying bird
> The ship sped on.

The Vikings are thought to have taken their beds with them on voyages. But because of their size—one bed found in a burial ship measured six feet by seven feet—they would have been dismantled and taken on board. The bed belonging to the leader was usually the largest and might be elaborately carved. The beds belonging to the crew and family members were simpler and more utilitarian. When the Vikings went ashore for the night, the beds were set up in the tents to make sleeping more comfortable.

Toward the end of the Viking era, the sagas describe large skin bags called *hudfat* that were used to store gear and weapons during the day. At night they were emptied and used as sleeping bags.

Vikings sometimes took their own beds on a voyage. This ornate headboard piece probably belonged to a chieftain.

COOKING IN CAMP

If cooking was to be done when the boat put into shore for the night, basic ingredients such as flour must have been stored on the ship. Flour used to make bread or porridge would have been ground using hand mills before the voyage began. The ground flour was kneaded into bread dough in wooden troughs. When the dough was ready to be cooked, it was put on small round pans and placed near the fire. The pans were mounted on long handles with a rivet in the middle, allowing the pan to be turned so the bread would bake evenly.

Liquids were cooked in pots, kettles, or cauldrons. The kettles could be hung by chains over fires. Metal pots were made of riveted iron or from copper sheets hammered into a round shape. Others were carved from soapstone. Soapstone is a rock that can be carved and shaped using a strong blade and a great deal of patience. The stone pots were popular, possibly because the stone retained heat for a long time, and they would have been less expensive than metal ones. Many soapstone pots have been found. An average pot held seven to eleven pints of liquid.

Wooden ladles were used for stirring and for ladling liquid out of the pots. They were usually carved from a single piece of wood and looked much like the ladles used today.

HOW ODIN DISCOVERED THE SECRET OF WRITING

In the popular saga *Havamal,* Odin sacrifices himself to learn the secret of writing. After nine nights of hanging himself in a tree, Odin discovers the runic alphabet. Bertil Almgren quotes a portion of the saga in *The Viking.*

I'm aware that I hung
on the windy tree,
Swung there nights all of nine;
gashed with a blade
bloodied for Odin
myself and offering to myself
knotted to that tree
no man knows
whither the root of it runs.

None gave me bread
none gave me drink
down to the depths I peered
to snatch up the runes
with a roaring scream
and fall in a dizzied faint.

Wellbeing I won
and Wisdom too,
I grew and joyed in my growth;
from a word to a word
I was led to a word
from a deed to another deed.

The Viking men hunted for meat for supper or the women cooked fish that were caught before the ship was put in for the night. Sometimes meat and fish were boiled, but grilling on forks or spits seems to have been popular. The women used large forks to lift the meat or fish from the cooking pots.

VIKING UTENSILS

Everyone, even the children, had their own knife to use at the table. Almost everything was eaten with their fingers once it was cut into manageable pieces. For liquids, the Vikings had spoons carved out of wood, horn, or antler. The food was eaten from wooden plates or platters, some of which have been found in the burial ships. They also had wooden bowls and trays.

Vikings who could not afford wooden plates, such as the thralls, may have eaten their food from slabs of stale bread, as was the custom in medieval Europe. Madeleine Pelner Cosman, a noted authority on medieval cooking, gives the following description: "Food . . . [was] placed before them upon large slices of bread, round in shape or, more usually, square, called 'trenchers.'"[29] After the main dish was eaten, the "plate" could be consumed as well.

The cooking implements used by the Vikings were the type that had been known for centuries, such as a collapsible tripod that was used to hang a kettle over a fire. The three legs were fastened at one end so it could be opened and spread over the flame. The weight of the kettle, as well as the points on the opposite end of the legs, kept the tripod from folding up or falling over. Kettles were suspended from iron chains that had loops at intervals so the pot could be raised from the heat or brought closer to it.

Fires were started by striking flint against palm-sized "steels." These pieces of metal were of a size to be carried and handled easily and had curling decorations similar to the carved prows of the dragon ships. Sparks would fly when the steels were struck with a piece of flint. Dry tinder would be ready to catch the sparks, and soon a small fire would be burning. Larger pieces of wood would be added to increase the size and intensity of the fire.

Light would also be needed when camping at night. Lamps were made from iron and had a cup for burning tallow or fish oil. The wick was made from moss. The lower end of the lamp was a pointed pole. Before lighting the fire, the point would have been shoved into the ground. At home, the lamp would have been stuck in the dirt or clay floors of the house. Like everything else, the lamps, when not in use, fit neatly into the sea chests.

WOODEN ITEMS

On shipboard, utensils and articles not in use were kept in wooden chests and boxes. These hinged boxes had intricate locks and keys were required to open them. Many of the chests were the perfect height and length to be used as a rowing bench on the ship. Some of the boxes that have been found contained only enough metal in their structure to keep them together. Others were strongboxes wrapped with iron and must have been used to safeguard valuables. The keys to all of the boxes were hung on the wife's belt as a symbol of her status as housewife. If a man denied his wife the keys of his household, according to Old Norse law, she could divorce him.

In addition to being skilled seamen and ferocious warriors, Vikings were also highly skilled artisans. This figure from a bowl is an example of some of their work.

The Vikings used large wooden buckets for brewing beer or storing salted meat. A small one found on a burial ship contained weaving tools and had a top that could be locked. An elaborate bucket on the Oseberg ship had sides that slanted in toward the top, and the curved handle was held in place by enameled figures of little men.

Troughs, used for serving food and kneading dough, were cut from single pieces of wood. Even though they were intended for daily use, they were elaborately decorated with designs that were carved on the ends and served as handles.

Although life at sea was less comfortable than it must have been in their homes on land, Vikings and their families were used to living under such conditions. Their love of adventure evidently made the privations worth the inconveniences.

EXPLORATION AND TRADE

The Vikings were great traders and explorers. During the ninth and tenth centuries, they sailed throughout the known world and also reached many previously unknown lands. Their voyages were driven by a desire for trade and a curiosity about what lay beyond the horizon. Adept at both sailing and navigating, the Vikings usually reached their destination, but sometimes their journeys took them in unpredictable directions.

Vikings from throughout Scandinavia journeyed around the globe. Vikings from Denmark sailed from the great trade city of Birka in Sweden, through the Baltic Sea, and into the North Sea. From there they traveled south past Germany, France, and Spain, and in the eleventh century their Norman descendants finally crossed into the Mediterranean Sea and on to Italy. Norwegian Vikings traveled to Scotland, England, Ireland, then beyond to Iceland, Greenland, and North America. Meanwhile, Vikings from Sweden traveled east across the Baltic Sea and down rivers into Russia, across the Caspian Sea and as far south as Baghdad, and across the Black Sea to Constantinople and up to Kiev.

THE VIKINGS AS SEAMEN

Vikings had exceptional navigational skills as well as a keen desire to simply explore. In *Barbarian Europe,* Gerald Simons describes their abilities.

The Northmen were superb shipwrights and ship handlers, and skillful navigators as well. Ship captains had records of landmarks as far west as Greenland; on the open sea they read the sun and stars with crude sighting devices to hold a given course. Few European sailors of the time ventured far from land; the Vikings, however, crossed the ocean to Ireland, Iceland, Greenland—and nearly 4,000 miles to the New World.

At times these trading trips had unexpected outcomes. The Viking traders who reached Russia, for instance, settled there. The leader, named Rurik, is believed to be the head of what became Russia's royal family.

Viking trade and exploration was made possible by the longship. The Vikings relied on their longships to carry them

The versatile longship allowed the Vikings to navigate rivers as well as open ocean. Swedish Vikings under Rurik sailed east and colonized what is now Russia. It is believed that the Russian royal line started with him.

safely from port to port, ferrying valuable cargo and introducing them to lands and cultures they had never before known.

THE BUILDING OF CARGO SHIPS

The longships sailed by Viking traders around A.D. 1000 were broader, deeper, and longer than warships. A longship of this sort was intended to carry large shipments of cargo over long distances and to be more stable in the water than the sleeker, faster warships. Except for the size, the design was still recognizable as a longship, having pointed and carved prows and sterns, a single steer board, and oarlocks for the oars along both sides.

Some records indicate that the great cargo ships were as large as 230 feet long. Many historians have questioned the accuracy of these accounts, citing Viking shipbuilding methods to support their contentions. One such ship, that of Canute the Great, was reputed to contain 60 *spantrum,* as the spaces between the deck beams were called. In a ship this large, the oar holes would have had to be 3 feet apart for the oarsmen to use the oars properly. This would have resulted in a weak hull, given the methods of shipbuilding that were assumed to have been used at that time.

THE ROSKILDE LONGSHIP

In the autumn of 1997, however, Danish archaeologists unearthed a longship in the mud of Roskilde harbor during a dredging project. The ship was the largest longship ever found, and it made historians rethink their estimates of the size of Viking cargo ships.

As archaeologist John R. Hale, an expert on Bronze Age Scandinavian boat design, states, "With its immense length of 35 meters [115 feet], the Roskilde longship surpasses all previous longship finds."[30] Although it is a warship, not one used for trade, its immense size suggests that cargo ships also might have exceeded previous size estimates. With ships this large, it would be possible to establish trade routes far from home, gathering goods from many countries along the way.

THE VIKINGS AS TRADERS

While some of the Vikings were traders, they were not as peaceful as the name implies. They were armed against pirates, and if

LOADING THE CARGO

Despite the great size of the longships, it was sometimes simpler to bring the ship to the cargo than the cargo to the ship. If the cargo was carried to the ship, it would mean transferring it from a smaller boat to the longship anchored in deeper water. Expensive goods could have been ruined or lost if they were dropped between boat and ship. So the ships were brought out of the water and loaded on the beach.

Once the goods were stowed safely on board, the ship was returned to the water. The usual way of accomplishing this was to cut down trees and use the trunks as rollers under the ship. Forests were usually close at hand and the Vikings could cut whatever was needed. The oars were placed inside the ship, the steering oar was hung from the gunwale by a hawser, or strong rope, so it would not be in the way. Then the crew pushed the ship forward on the rollers or used horses to drag it. As the ship passed over the tree trunks, the Vikings took the logs from the stern and carried them to the bow to be used again.

they happened upon a cargo-laden ship less defended than their own, they would sometimes turn pirate themselves and steal the cargo. If the inhabitants of a country were unwilling to trade, the Vikings often turned raiders and took whatever they pleased.

Since Sweden faced east on the Baltic Sea, it was natural for these Vikings to sail across what is now northern Russia and travel south down the Volga and Dnieper Rivers. The Swedish Vikings were especially gifted traders and established trading posts at towns such as Novgorod and Kiev. When they returned to their homeland, the Vikings brought pelts from otter, marten, and beaver; amber for jewelry; walrus ivory; honey; and furs from Russian territories farther to the north. They also brought slaves captured in raids from other countries, and they returned with exotic goods from Constantinople, Baghdad, and other Muslim cities in the East.

One of the major trading centers was Birka, an island in Lake Mälaren in eastern Sweden. German, Frisian, and Frankish traders came there as well as Anglo-Saxons from England. Gerald Simons reports that these traders brought "glassware, woolen cloth, sword blades and other Western manufactures for silver and spices from Arabia, exquisite Byzantine brocades, ornamented leatherwork from Persia."[31]

Birka was the perfect location for a trade center. Few people lived on the island, and it did not belong exclusively to any area, yet was located close enough for the king of Sweden to protect it. In return for his protection, the king was allowed to purchase new imports three days before they were offered to anyone else. A sheltering archipelago also protected Birka from the sea and its dangers of raiders and storms.

Norway had only one trading town, Kaupang. Today the bay is shallow and the surrounding land is too marshy for the location to seem likely as a busy trade center. But in the Vikings' day, the bay was much deeper, and Kaupang was a port with excellent harboring facilities.

THE COUNTRIES VISITED BY VIKINGS

Although not as skilled at trading as the Swedes, Vikings from other parts of Scandinavia had an insatiable desire to see what was beyond the horizon. Norwegian Vikings, who lived on the west side of Scandinavia, sailed into the Atlantic Ocean to explore, colonize, and trade. As Simons writes,

> In the Ninth Century they colonized the largely uninhabited islands of Iceland, the Faeroes, the Hebrides and Orkneys, and occupied half of Ireland, as well as large areas of Scotland and northwestern England. During the 10th Century they set up bases in Greenland and reached the shores of North America around 1000.[32]

The Vikings from Denmark were less isolated than the rest of Scandinavia because they lived on a peninsula rising out of what is now Germany. It was easier for them to concentrate their raids on and trade with Frankish countries and eastern England.

OTTAR'S AMAZING VOYAGE

One of the most famous Viking explorers was a man from Norway named Ottar, who lived late in the ninth century. He is credited with compiling the first accurate description of the geography of the northern coast of Europe, a place that had never been seen by humans. Ottar had a great curiosity about the region to the north of his homeland.

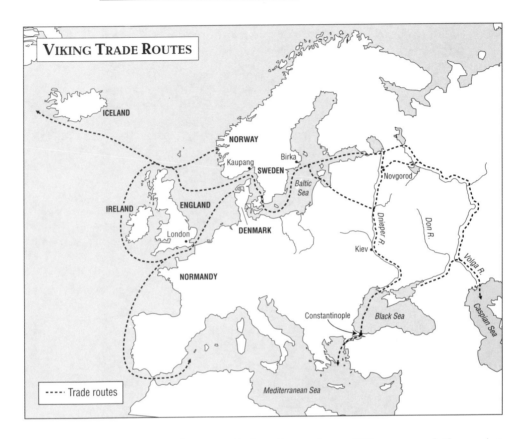

After sailing north for three days, Ottar passed the point where Scandinavian whale hunters usually turned back. For another three days he followed a rocky coastline. When the coast turned east, Ottar sailed for four more days, using favorable winds to drive his longship. After the fourth day, the coast turned south and Ottar followed it to a river. After going farther south down the river, he encountered the first group of people since starting his journey. The people were not friendly and did not want to trade, so Ottar turned around and sailed home.

Ottar had only been satisfying his curiosity, but he was the first man to discover the northernmost coastline of Europe, which is now called North Cape. His voyage took him through the part of the Arctic Ocean known as the Barents Sea, then southward into the White Sea. The river he found may have been either the Dvina or the Onega River in what is now northern Russia. Although the same voyage would later be made by well-equipped whaler ships and Russian icebreakers, Ottar made the journey in an open longship, using only a single sail and rowers to propel him. Simply surviving the harsh weather and fierce storms was a remarkable feat.

THE COLONIZATION OF ICELAND

Viking explorers also discovered Iceland, a large island in the North Atlantic. On two separate voyages, Vikings had seen the island; although they did not explore it, they did tell others of their discovery. Tales of these two voyages reached a Viking explorer named Floki, who went there only to see what he might discover. He sailed in the direction that the other two ships had taken and found the island by releasing ravens and following them as they headed for land. Because of the ice storms during the winter that Floki spent there, he named the place Iceland. When he returned to Norway and told others what he had seen, several families set out to colonize the island.

Toward the end of the ninth century, one of those families bore a son who, because of the color of his hair, came to be known as Erik the Red. After he killed a man, Erik the Red was banished from his home in Iceland.

By Scandinavian law, someone who committed a crime was banished from his homeland for at least three years; for worse crimes, the banishment lasted an entire lifetime. An outlaw lost all his

Erik the Red slays an Icelandic chieftain. Erik was banished from Iceland and sailed west to form a colony on what is now Greenland.

possessions and anyone who saw him was permitted to kill him.

Erik the Red set sail aboard a longship, heading west toward a land other Vikings had seen but never explored.

THE COLONIZATION OF GREENLAND

Erik landed his longship on what is now Cape Farewell, the southernmost tip of Greenland. After traveling up a fjord and finding fertile land, Erik named the country Greenland to encourage other Vikings to settle there. Unfortunately, the colonists who arrived in 985 discovered that there was little green to be found. The colony, however, survived for over four centuries.

The fate of the Greenland colony remains a mystery. While a supply ship was sent annually from Norway, all was well; after a time, however, the ship stopped coming and the colony died out. Some think the local Eskimos, who were usually friendly, may have killed them. Others believe the harsh weather caused the sparse vegetation to die out and the colonists died of malnutrition. Graves found in modern times contain skeletons of adult men under five feet tall and women barely taller than four feet. Their small size would indicate extreme malnutrition.

THE DISCOVERY OF VINLAND

Long before the colony reached such dire straits, Erik the Red and his wife had a son named Leif Eriksson, called Leif the Lucky. Historians believe that Leif is one of the two Vikings to reach the northeast coast of North America around the year 1000. Leif named the land he discovered Vinland.

The *Flatey Book,* which was written late in the fourteenth century, tells of a Viking trader and longship captain named Bjarni Herjulfson, who reached North America even before the voyage of Leif Eriksson. Bjarni was the captain of a longship and

NAVIGATION USING LANDMARKS

King Alfred the Great of Wessex, England, ordered a translation of Orosius's *Universal History.* In it, Ottar, a Norwegian merchant, mentions Kaupang, which he calls Sciringesheal. This account, related in *The Vikings* by Frank R. Donovan, shows how the Vikings must have used landmarks to navigate through unknown waters.

Ottar related that the district in which he lived is called Halgoland. No one, he said, lived farther north than he. But there is a port in the southern end of the country. This port people called Sciringesheal, and to it, he said, one could not sail in less than a month if one camped by night and had favourable winds by day. And one must ever sail along by the land. And Ireland will be on the starboard side, and then the islands which are between Ireland and this country [England]. Then it is this country till one comes to Sciringesheal. And all the way on the port side is Norway. South of Sciringesheal a large sea runs up into the country. The sea is wider there than any man can see across.

The remains of Brattahlid, the eastern settlement on Greenland. Though there was no farmable land in Greenland, Viking settlements lasted for four centuries.

a trader by profession. Every year he came home to Iceland to spend the winter with his father. One year, upon his return he learned that his father had moved to Greenland. Bjarni had never been to Greenland, but he knew it was west of Iceland, and he sailed away, confident that he would find it. Bjarni and his men sailed for three days before getting lost in a fog. When the sun reappeared, they sailed on, not knowing where they were. Three times land was sighted, but Bjarni knew that it could not be Greenland because there were no fjords or mountains. Historians believe the lands he saw are the ones later named Labrador, Newfoundland, and North America. At last, a gale blew them north and they finally saw Greenland, a land with snow-capped mountains.

According to the saga,

> They directed their course thither and landed in the evening below a cape on which there was a boat, and there upon this cape dwelt Herjulf, Bjarni's father. Bjarni now went to his father, gave up his voyaging and remained with his father while Herjulf lived.[33]

LEIF ERIKSSON'S DISCOVERY

Tales of Bjarni's voyage and sightings reached Iceland and captured the interest of Leif Eriksson. Eriksson bought Bjarni's longship, found a willing crew, and set sail in 1000. According to the saga (as told in both the *Flatey Book* and *Hauk's Book*),

> There they sailed up to the land, and having cast anchor and lowered a boat, went ashore and saw no grass there. The background was all great glaciers, and the intermediate land from the sea to the glaciers was like one flat rock, and the country seemed to them destitute of value. Then Leif said, "We have not failed to land, like Bjarni; now I will give this country a name and call it 'Helluland.'" [34]

Helluland means "land of flat stone." Historians believe he landed at Baffin Island off the northeast coast of Canada.

The saga continues:

> Thereupon they returned on board, after which they sailed to sea and discovered the second land. Again they sailed up to the land and lowered a boat and went ashore. This land was low-lying and wooded, and wherever they went there were wide stretches of white sand, and the slope from the sea was not abrupt. Then Leif said, "This land shall be given a name from its resources and shall be called Markland." [35]

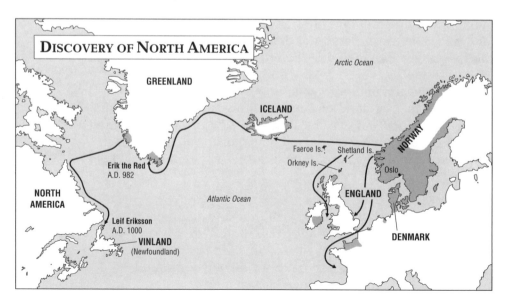

DISCOVERY OF NORTH AMERICA

Almost five hundred years before Columbus set sail, Leif Eriksson landed on what is to-day Newfoundland. There is evidence that Leif set up a colony in North America at the beginning of the eleventh century.

This word means "Woodland." Evidence has been discovered at L'Anse aux Meadows, a small village on the cape of Newfoundland, of a Viking settlement that has been dated to Leif Eriksson's lifetime. It is believed that Leif must have landed there during his discovery voyage and that a settlement was later founded there.

According to the saga, Leif's adventure was not finished:

> After which they returned to the ship as quickly as possible. And they sailed after that in the open sea with a northeast wind and were out two days before they saw land, toward which they sailed and . . . cast anchor, and carrying their leather kitbags ashore, they put up shelters, but, later on, deciding to pass the winter there, they made large houses.[36]

Leif named the new country Vinland (or Wine-Land) because he found an abundance of wild grapes that the Vikings could use to make wine. The only place grapes could have grown wild at this time was North America, although the exact location of his landing is unknown.

THE VOYAGES OF LEIF'S BROTHERS AND SISTER

After Leif returned to Greenland, his brother Thorvald also decided to explore the new land. Because longships were difficult to build, they continued to be used as long as they were seaworthy, often changing hands several times. So Thorvald took over Bjarni's longship and sailed west to Vinland. The new expedition wintered in Vinland at Leif's camp. The following spring they explored the coastline, and Thorvald found a headland where he intended to make his new home.

As Thorvald and his crew were returning to their ship after exploring the headland, they encountered the native inhabitants, whom they called Skraelings, meaning "wretches." The Vikings attacked the Skraelings (or Indians, as later explorers called them) and killed all but one. The next morning, the Skraeling who had escaped returned with a war party and attacked the Northmen. The only casualty noted was Thorvald. Before he died, Thorvald, who had converted to Christianity, asked that he be buried on the headland and that the place be called Crossness. He was the first Viking buried in the New World.

Erik the Red's third son, Thorstein, also set sail for Vinland but never reached it. Upon returning to Greenland, Thorstein died.

Others were also drawn to the wonderful new land where grass and woodlands were plentiful and game was abundant. Thorstein's widow, Gudrid, and her new husband, Thorfinn Karlsefni, joined Erik the Red's daughter, Freydis, and her husband, Thorvard, along with three longships and a company of men to make the voyage to Vinland in the spring of 1009.

THE COLONIZATION OF VINLAND

They found Helluland (probably Baffin Island) and Markland (probably Newfoundland), and after following the coastline, they discovered a place to land. They moored their longships in a bay Thorfinn named Straumfjord and settled in for the summer. It was here that Gudrid gave birth to a son, whom they named Snorri.

The winter lasted longer and was stormier and colder than the Vikings expected, and they were soon running low on food.

THE VOYAGE OF LEIF AND HIS FAMILY

Sometimes Vikings set out on voyages out of necessity. These voyages sometimes led to the exploration and colonization of new countries.

In 874 a Viking named Leif and his foster brother, Ingolf, killed two young sons of Viking noblemen. Because Leif started the fatal fight, he was outlawed in his home country of Norway, which meant he lost everything he owned there. With nothing to hold them to Norway, Leif and Ingolf decided to immigrate to Iceland, an island that had been discovered by other Vikings who had been blown off course by storms.

The two brothers went to Iceland, liked what they saw, and prepared to move there. While Ingolf went back to Norway to pack his belongings, Leif went on a raid to Ireland to steal gold, silver, and enough slaves to do the work of settling in the new country.

When Leif returned to Norway, as Frank R. Donovan records in *The Vikings,* the brothers loaded their

> two ships with household goods, cattle, their wives and relatives, and a small band of free-men. Ingolf took with him the pillars of the high seat in his hall, which were carved with sacred Viking images. When he neared the coast of Iceland, he cast these [pillars] overboard, vowing to settle wherever the gods caused them to drift onto the beach. The gods made a good choice by washing the pillars ashore near Iceland's present capital, Reykjavik.

It is unknown where Leif landed. His Irish slaves revolted, murdered the Vikings, and took the women to a nearby island. Ingolf discovered what had happened and began searching for them. When they were found, he killed the slaves and rescued the women. He blamed the ill luck that befell Leif on his brother not having abided by the gods' choice of a landing place.

Viking expeditions were not always staged to sack prosperous villages. Vikings were sometimes forced to leave home because of legal trouble. Such expeditions often laid the foundation for new colonies.

They moved from the mainland to an island where there was better grazing for the cattle they had brought on the voyage, but by midwinter they faced the possibility of starvation.

When the weather warmed, an old man named Thorhall the Hunter took one of the three ships and set sail for Greenland with a group of colonists who chose not to stay in Vinland. A storm blew them off course and they never reached their destination. According to the sagas, they ended up as slaves in Ireland.

THE END OF THORFINN'S EXPEDITION

The rest of Thorfinn's expedition sailed south and found the coast of what is now New England. Seeing that there were plentiful grapes, fish, game, and fields for grazing, they built a more permanent camp on a river they named Hop. About two weeks after they arrived, nine canoes full of Indians sailed down the river. After watching the Vikings for a while, the Indians, who were probably the ancestors of the Micmac or another Algonquin tribe, paddled away. In the spring the Indians returned and began to trade peacefully with the Vikings, bartering red cloth for pelts.

All went well until the day when a Viking's bull charged the Indians. Terrified, the Indians ran to their canoes and left in haste. Three weeks later the Indians returned armed for battle. The Vikings had built a protective wall around the camp, but the Indians caught them outside and unprotected. Freydis, who was a formidable woman, led the attack against the Indians and drove them away.

The Vikings returned to the more peaceful surroundings of Straumfjord, their original settlement. Here, during their third winter in America, quarrels broke out among the Vikings, some say over the women who had accompanied them on the voyage. The following spring, Thorfinn, along with Gudrid and little Snorri, returned to Greenland.

THE VIKINGS IN AMERICA

No one knows how far inland the Vikings may have traveled to build their colonies and explore. They had long since learned how to navigate the longships up rivers. The ships rode high in the water and did not need great depth to float. If the wind was not strong enough to fill the sails, the oars could carry the ship forward. If they encountered a waterfall, the ship could be taken ashore and carried beyond it.

Freydis, daughter of Erik the Red and sister to Leif Eriksson, helped fight off a vicious Indian attack on their North American settlement. She and her husband eventually returned to Greenland.

One intriguing piece of evidence suggests that the Vikings may actually have reached what is today the northern United States. In 1898 a farmer found a stone covered with runes on his Minnesota farm. The Kensington Stone, as it is called, tells the story of a Viking expedition to Vinland in 1362, in which ten men were killed by Indians. This type of stone was frequently erected by loved ones or devoted followers to mark the site of a battle or the death of an important person. No one seems able to agree if the Kensington Stone is proof that the Vikings penetrated all the way to present day Minnesota or if the stone is simply an elaborate hoax.

The Kensington Stone tells the story of a Viking expedition to North America in the late–fourteenth century. The stone was found in a field in Minnesota in 1898.

There are other mentions of voyages to Vinland. In 1121 a bishop named Erik Gnupsson sailed there, and in 1347 a cargo of larch wood arrived in Iceland from the forests of Markland. Coffins and other items made from the wood of American trees have been excavated over the years in Viking graves. There is no explanation why the Vikings abandoned a country of such rich resources. Perhaps they were dissatisfied because they were far from other countries that could be raided and too far removed from the lucrative trade routes. Vikings never seemed to be happy unless there was the prospect of returning to the sea.

WARFARE AND CONQUEST

In only two hundred years the Vikings had discovered and started colonies on virtually every island between Scandinavia and North America. Early in the ninth century they had invaded Britain and the countries along the western and northern shores of Europe. The primary attacks on England were by Danes, or Vikings from Denmark. In 793 they raided a monastery at Lindisfarne in Northumbria, soon after, a monastery south of there at Jarrow.

The ninth-century scholar Aleuin wrote a letter to the king of Northumbria, Athelred the Unready, bemoaning the fact that, in 350 years,

A group of Danish Vikings prepares for a raid on Britain. Britain and Ireland were a favorite target for the savage Norsemen.

never before has such a terror appeared in Britain as we
have now suffered from a pagan race, nor was it thought
that such an inroad from the sea could be made. Behold,
the church of St. Cuthbert spattered with the blood of the
priests of God, despoiled of all its ornaments, a place
more venerable than all in Britain is given as a prey to
pagan people.[37]

Attacks such as this are described in detail in the yearly Anglo-
Saxon chronicles, which were probably begun in the late ninth
century by monks who may have lived in Winchester, England.
For the year 793, the chronicles recorded:

In this year fierce, foreboding omens came over the land
of Northumbria, and wretchedly terrified the people.
There were excessive whirlwinds, lightning storms, and
fiery dragons were seen flying in the sky. These signs
were followed by great famine, and shortly after in the
same year, on January 8th, the ravaging of heathen men
[Vikings] destroyed God's church at Lindisfarne through
brutal robbery and slaughter.[38]

At about the same time as the attack on Lindisfarne, another
raid was reported on England's southern coast. As another
chronicle precisely reports,

When the very pious king Brihtric was ruling over the
domains of the east Saxons, . . . suddenly a not very
large fleet of the Danes arrived, speedy vessels to the
number of three; that was their first arrival. At the re-
port, the king's reeve (a royal official with duties like a
steward) who was then in the town called Dorchester,
leapt on his horse, sped to the harbour with a few men
(for he thought they were merchants rather than ma-
rauders) and admonishing them in an authoritative
manner gave orders that they should be driven to the
royal town. And he and his companions were killed by
them on the spot.[39]

THE VALUE OF THE LONGSHIPS IN THE RAIDS

The Vikings were so successful at their raids because they were
able to arrive silently and swiftly. Although the longships grew
larger as the years passed and new innovations were made,

they remained relatively lightweight. Historian John R. Hale writes that they were hewn by a broad ax from

> local oak cut from 300-year-old trees in lengths exceeding 10 meters [33 feet] without a knot or blemish. . . . They pared the planking to a thickness of two centimeters [less than 1 inch]—a finger's breadth—and trimmed every sliver of excess wood from the rib frames.[40]

Because of the ships' remarkably shallow draft, Hale goes on to say the Vikings were able to "approach almost any beach or to invade deep inland via a waterway only a few meters [yards] deep. The more than 60 warriors on the largest ships could jump over the low side of the hull within a few strides of land."[41] The light weight of the longship enabled one Viking, King Magnus Barelegs of Norway, to take advantage of a legal loophole. Hale relates the story:

> A treaty with the king of Scotland granted Magnus all the land he could circumnavigate in his ship. The Norseman sailed to the Scottish peninsula of Kintyre and, sitting at the rudder, had his men drag him across the narrow neck of land so he could claim it.[42]

RIDING HIGH IN THE WATER

In *The Viking*, Bertil Almgren explains why the Vikings were able to conduct their raids so successfully.

> Although Viking ships were of approximately the same size as a modern small schooner, their keels were usually less than forty inches below the waterline. In ships like these, landing on beaches or penetrating far up inland waterways presented no difficulties. Not many minutes need have elapsed from the time a Viking ship was first sighted through the North Sea haze to the time when the pirates were ashore in the coastal towns and villages, plundering and killing. By the time the defenders had assembled, the raiders would be well away with their booty, rowing for all they were worth against the strong head-wind which made such sailing vessels as their pursuers might have had quite useless.

VIKING BATTLE GEAR

The Vikings may have been the first warriors to dress in armor. Frank R. Donovan describes the Viking battle dress:

> a short coat of chain mail worn over a long woolen shirt gathered at the waist by a leather belt. Over that was a cloak of wool or animal skin clasped with an elaborately carved brooch. . . . [On his head he wore] a simple metal hat with nose and cheek guards. . . . He may have carried a thrusting spear about eleven feet long or several light throwing spears. His sword was slung over his shoulder and hung down his back. He had an axe and probably a short, single-edged knife thrust through his belt. In his left hand he carried a round shield.[43]

The Vikings were among the first warriors to make use of body armor.

Vikings were fond of jewelry and often wore carved armbands or bracelets made of silver.

Several types of spears were used. Long, heavy ones were for thrusting, smaller ones for throwing. There were iron pikes and halberds, which were a combination of spear and ax with a long handle. The spearheads were made in various shapes, from long and slim to short and wide. Some resembled harpoons, arrowheads, or fish spears. Those with teeth pointing backwards were meant to cause more damage when they were pulled out than when they were thrust in.

The Viking's pride was his sword. The most common kind was broad, with a double-edged blade. Others, called *scramasax*, were more narrow and had a single edge. Both kinds had straight blades, and most had decorations on their handles, sheaths, and blades. According to Donovan, Viking warriors gave their swords exciting names such as Gleam of Battle, Serpent of the Wound, Fire of the Sea Kings, and Thorn of the Shields.

The chain mail armor was called the *brynja*, and it was made from flexible iron rings. Although the sagas refer to plate armor, none has been found. The helmets were simple, cone-shaped hats made of metal with nose guards. Although carvings show Vikings in helmets with horns or made in the likeness of bear or wolf heads, these must have been worn only for ceremonial show by kings or chieftains.

Sagas mention shields long enough to carry a dead warrior's body, but the only shields that have been found are round and about three feet in diameter. They were wooden and sometimes covered with leather. Often they were painted. In the center of the shield, a raised knob of bronze or iron passed through and was shaped into a handle on the back.

The Vikings were fond of jewelry and were quite skilled at making beautiful pieces like this brooch.

THE VIKINGS IN BATTLE

The Vikings succeeded in their raids because they were seasoned warriors and because those they attacked were usually only farmers with no training and only crude weapons. Kings had no standing armies and maintained only a small group of bodyguards. The Vikings had the added advantage of controlling the sea. If the battle started to go wrong, they had only to retreat to the longships and sail away. The monks or farmers they were attacking had no way to follow them.

Battle strategy was a Viking strong point. They even practiced tactics in their games of chess. One of the favorite battle formations was based on the shape of a wedge, or triangle. Donovan describes the Vikings in battle:

> Each leader was the point of a wedge and was covered by his shieldman. Other fighters were formed fanlike behind the point, each man armed with a long spear and an axe or a sword. Several of these wedges might be placed side-by-side, touching at the bases. Behind them slingers, javelin throwers, and archers were arrayed in lines, and in addition there were rows of replacements for men in the wedges.[44]

Sometimes the Vikings pretended to retreat from the men they were fighting. The men would run after them, not bothering to stay in their own battle formations, only to have the Vikings regroup unexpectedly and defeat them. In battle, the Vikings were fiercely loyal to their leader and had unwavering discipline; turning and running from a fight would mean they would be excluded from Valhalla when they died. No Valkyries would come for a coward, and they would not be allowed to fight forever beside Odin. While dying, a Viking would chant a list of the brave battles in which he had fought so the Valkyries would know he was worthy of Odin's army.

Vikings were seasoned warriors, and their mastery of the sea gave them a distinct strategic advantage.

THE ATTACK ON LUNA, ITALY

Not all Viking victories came about by means of outright warfare. Sometimes deviousness was necessary.

Bjorn Ironside and a Viking leader named Hastings set out to conquer Rome. After plundering Pisa, they neared the city of Luna, which they apparently mistook for Rome. Luna was so heavily fortified that the Vikings soon discovered they had little chance of taking the city in a forthright battle. Therefore, they called a truce and sent word to the city that one of their leaders was dying and wanted to be baptized as a Christian. Priests came out and baptized Hastings, then returned to their walled city.

The next day Bjorn sent word that Hastings had died during the night and asked permission to bury him in hallowed ground inside the city. The gates were opened for the mourners and funeral procession to enter. Once there were enough Vikings in the gates to hold them open, Hastings jumped from his coffin, sword in hand, and started killing the inhabitants of Luna. The other Vikings rushed in, and soon the city was theirs.

WARRIOR WOMEN

Viking women were also warriors when the occasion called for it. According to the *Flatey Book,* during Thorfinn's 1009 expedition to Vinland (now known as North America), Erik the Red's daughter, Freydis, led an attack on the inhabitants.

The last recorded voyage to Vinland was of two longships, one sailed by Freydis and her husband and the other, larger one by two brothers. Despite the agreement Freydis had made with the brothers before the voyage, she smuggled five extra men onto her longship. Freydis was determined to be leader of the encampment. Although the brothers arrived in Vinland first and had moved into the house that her brother, Leif Eriksson, had left behind, Freydis made them move out by claiming her brother had loaned the house to her and her husband, Thorvard.

When things did not go her way, Freydis told her husband that she had been insulted by the two brothers and forced Thorvard to overpower the men. She ordered her men to kill both brothers and all of their men. She also ordered them to kill all the women. When her own men refused to carry out her order, Freydis killed the women herself. After threatening to kill anyone who told what she had done, she had all the supplies loaded onto the larger ship (the one that had belonged to the brothers) and sailed back to Greenland.

BERSERKERS

When in battle, the Vikings were sometimes consumed by a frenzy in which they apparently felt no pain and had a superhuman strength. In this state, the warriors were known as berserkers. When they were in this frenzy, they would throw aside their shields and chain mail and start killing the enemy without regard for their own safety.

A story was told of a man who had twelve sons:

> They were all great berserkers. They went on warfare when they were quite young and ravaged far and wide, but met with no equal in strength and courage. . . . It was their custom, if they were with only their own men when they found the *berserks gang* [berserk fury] coming over them, to go ashore and wrestle with large stones or trees, otherwise in their rage they would have slain their friends.[45]

IVAR THE BONELESS VERSUS ATHELRED THE UNREADY

Even without the berserker fury, the Vikings were a formidable enemy. With their advanced battle strategies and fearlessness of death, they did not hesitate to take whatever they wanted. At first the Vikings attacked England only to get precious metals such as gold and silver, as well as jewels, slaves, and anything else of value. Eventually, however, they began to claim land as their own. In the middle of the ninth century, the Danish Vikings banded together to form the Great Army, a military force to invade England.

The general of the Great Army was a Viking named Ivar the Boneless, son of Ragnar Lodbrok (which means "Hairy Britches"), who was one of the greatest Viking leaders of the ninth century. In 865 Ivar and his army landed in East Anglia and attacked the forces led by the English king. Following the king's death, Athelred the Unready became the new king. *Unready* is a mistranslation of the Anglo-Saxon word *redeless*, which meant "ill-advised." His younger brother, Alfred, was one of his best generals. Their troops met the Vikings in 871 in the hills near Ashdown in Wessex, England. The battle brought a

Vikings under a chieftain named Rollo terrorized France to such an extent that they were eventually offered all of what is today Normandy if they let the French live in peace.

rare defeat for the Vikings. Shortly afterward, Athelred became ill and died; Alfred, later to be called "the Great," became king.

ALFRED THE GREAT AGAINST THE VIKINGS

Although his people were united, King Alfred's men were out-numbered and weary from fighting. Alfred made a peace offering

WARSHIPS AND MERCHANTMEN

The differences between the merchant longships and those intended for warfare is explained by Bertil Almgren in *The Viking*.

> Warships, . . . obviously had to be built for speed, with or without wind. They had places for many oarsmen, and were, in fact, most often used in sheltered coastal waters, where seaworthiness was not as essential as it was in the case of merchantmen.
>
> No one knows when the distinction between merchantman and warship first began to be made, but by about 1000 A.D. an established difference existed. It seems reasonable to associate the origin of a special type of ship intended for commerce with the growth of the first towns. Obviously, too, there must have been a period when shipbuilders tried to combine warlike and commercial vessels in a single vessel. The Gokstad ship, for example, is probably one that had not yet acquired a distinct character, one that could be used as warship and which could also carry sufficient cargo to make sea transportation profitable.

in the form of gold. The Vikings took the gold and agreed to leave Alfred and his people in peace; however, the Vikings returned every year and demanded more gold. The payment became known as *Danegeld*. Gerald Simons writes that the Anglo-Saxons continued to pay the price. They had a saying that went, "Buy off the spear aimed at your breast if you do not wish to feel its point,"[46] meaning it was better to give the Vikings gold than to be killed by them.

By 878 the Vikings moved onto the east coast of England, taking the land as their own. This territory became known as the Danelaw and covered much of central and eastern England.

King Alfred had to hide in marshes and forests to keep from being captured during the last Viking conquest of the ninth century, but he finally united his people with southern England. By this time Guthrum was king of most of the Danish Vikings, and in 886 he agreed to keep his Vikings within the boundary of the

Danelaw. Except for occasional clashes between 886 and 889, Alfred's reign was peaceful. The peace lasted until Alfred's death in 899. He was succeeded by his son Edward the Elder, but the country was again plagued by Viking attacks.

ROLLO AND CHARLES THE SIMPLE

Unlike the Vikings ruled by Guthrum, the Vikings in France were not bound to an area and were going farther and farther inland. One group of Frankish monks were driven from their monastery on the island of Noirmoutier at the mouth of the Loire River just prior to 858. One of the monks, a man named Ermentarius, wrote:

> The number of ships grows larger and larger, the great host of Northmen continually increases; on every hand Christians are the victims of massacres, looting, incendiarism, clear proof of which will remain as long as the world itself endures; they capture every city they pass through, and none can withstand them.[47]

The Vikings had learned that the monasteries and churches contained more riches than could be found collected together elsewhere.

The French king, Charles the Simple, was unable to control the Vikings. So he made an offer to a Viking named Rollo. Charles offered to give him a large amount of land where the Seine River met the sea in the hopes that Rollo would defend it as staunchly as he had despoiled that same area. Surprisingly, the plan worked.

Rollo was an odd choice as protector. He had recently retreated with haste from an attack on Chartres, which was a disgraceful act for a Viking. Legend has it that Rollo was sent scurrying because the bishop of Chartres climbed to the town battlements and waved a garment that was said to have been worn by the Virgin Mary on the night of Jesus' birth. By this time some of the Vikings had been exposed to Christianity from contact with Christians on their trade routes, and they may have feared heavenly retribution. Or they may have recognized the cloth as being some sort of holy relic from the manner in which it was presented, and they may have been superstitious of any object that was believed to bring holy vengeance upon them.

However, it is also possible—and more likely—that Rollo had learned that French troops were approaching. Whatever his reason for stopping the attack, Rollo seemed an unlikely person to defend France.

After acquiring the territory of Normandy, Rollo and his band of Vikings adopted the religion, language, and the manners of French society. They became some of the fiercest defenders of the French kingdom.

Rollo showed amazing loyalty to Charles, however, and quickly fit into French society. By 942 Rollo and other Vikings had married French women, become Christians, and spoke French rather than their own language. These Vikings became known as Normans, a contraction of the word *Northmen,* and the territory became known as Normandy. Rollo's great-great-grandson, William (also known as William the Conqueror), conquered England in 1066 at the Battle of Hastings.

The sagas add an intriguing note to the Battle of Hastings. Long before that battle took place, when Ivar the Boneless lay dying, he ordered that he be buried in a mound on the English shoreline. He promised that as long as his body lay undisturbed no enemy could land there. According to the saga,

> When Vilhjalm . . . [William the Conqueror] came ashore he went [to the burial site] and broke Ivar's [grave] mound and saw that his [Ivar's] body had not decayed. Then he had a large pyre made and Ivar burned on it. Thereupon he landed and got the victory.[48]

After this point in history, no other Vikings were able to conquer England. The time of the great Viking raids had passed.

6

THE VIKING LEGACIES

The age of the Vikings lasted less than three centuries. During that short span of time, they explored lands that Europeans never even knew existed. Their travels brought them as far as Iceland, Greenland, and North America. They established lasting trade routes from Scandinavia to Russia, Spain, Baghdad, and the holy land. They took riches and knowledge from the people they conquered, but they also introduced new ideas—about law, navigation, and shipbuilding—to the cultures with whom they came in contact. In Russia, for example, the Vikings established a royal family that ruled for generations.

The longship made all of this possible. For the first time a group of people had the means to sail quickly and efficiently across vast oceans, into narrow channels and sheltered bays, and even up rivers. Their ships could hold a fully armed crew as well as cattle and cargo. They could even be carried on land, if necessary.

The longship was vital to the success of the Vikings, but it could not keep their civilization alive. Though their fierce spirit enabled them to conquer many peoples, the Vikings often settled and merged with those whom they conquered. They married local women, learned the local language, and adopted local customs. In doing so, the Vikings brought about their own demise.

MERGING WITH OTHER CULTURES

Even the son of the Viking warrior queen Olga (who all but annihilated the Russian tribe of people called the Drevlyane Slavs to avenge the death of her husband, Igor) denounced the ways of his parents. Svyatoslav considered himself neither a Viking nor a Russian, but contemporary accounts show him to be Russian in his dress and appearance.

In Normandy, the Viking Rollo—who had been called Hrolf before settling in France—became a Frenchman. Frank R. Donovan points out the extent of this changeover in only two generations:

Rollo is baptized in France. Within two generations the Normans were more French in manner than Scandinavian.

When Rollo's grandson Richard talked of returning to Viking paganism, his thoroughly Christianized knights would have no part of it. These were no longer pagan Northmen; they had become completely French in dress, manners, language, customs, and religion. They stood guard to protect their new homeland from their old countrymen; after Rollo, France was forever free from new territorial conquests by Northmen.[49]

This is a mold for casting Christian crosses and Thor's hammers. The Vikings had little trouble blending Christianity with paganism.

The Vikings frequently converted to Christianity. Christian crosses found beside Thor's hammers show that the Vikings had no difficulty in combining Christianity and paganism. Although some Vikings probably developed a genuine belief in the teachings of Christianity, others adopted Christianity because it was good for business. Bertil Almgren explains this attitude: "If they wanted to do business with Christian merchants, some Scandinavian traders had to let themselves be signed with the Cross and declare themselves Christians, but they were not baptized, thereby avoiding offence to their own gods." [50]

VIKING INFLUENCE ON OTHER CULTURES

In addition to colonizing places such as Iceland and Greenland and establishing trade routes that benefited Europeans, the Vikings established a type of government known as feudalism. This government was based on the Scandinavian role model with serfs (or thralls) at the bottom of the social ladder and the king at the top. Europe developed rapidly under this type of government.

The Vikings also brought a system of law to the countries they invaded and settled. This law was based on the rule of the people rather than the rule of only the king.

VIKINGS AND THE LAW

During the reign of the Viking kings, England learned to live under Scandinavian law and adopted it as its own. This law system is also the basis for American law. In 1076 the historian Adam of Bremen said of the Icelanders, "They have no king; only law."[51]

Since ancient times Teutonic people (including the Vikings) have settled disputes at meetings called *things*. There, every free man had a right to speak in his defense and be heard. The republic founded in Iceland was a democracy or, to be more exact, an aristodemocracy, which means the leaders divided the power among themselves. Together they formed the Althing.

Almgren elaborates on the system:

What appeared to be a republic was a kind of interlocked family dynasty. Most of the chiefs who were given the greatest power at the foundation of the Althing are thought to have been either members of the same family or connected with it through marriage. . . . The country was divided into twelve, later thirteen, lesser *things* (a word which also meant jurisdictions), and there were three chiefs in each *thing.* These thirty-six (later thirty-nine) chiefs formed the legislative body of the Althing, where the laws were made, and so shared the supreme power between them.[52]

VIKING INFLUENCE ON SHIPBUILDING

A more concrete influence can be seen in developments in shipbuilding and the growth of naval powers, particularly along the coast of western Europe. After about 911 most of the French fleets of Normandy and the neighboring province of Britanny consisted of newly settled Vikings or Viking descendants. England also gained from its dealings with the Vikings. England's long-running dominance of the seas had its beginnings in Viking seamanship learned during Viking raids and passed on to later generations.

Ship development also owes much to Viking longship design. Thanks to extensive contact between Vikings and other peoples, many cultures adopted the Viking style of shipbuilding. As naval historian Guy R. Williams writes,

THE DISCOVERY OF A VIKING SETTLEMENT

In *The Vikings,* Frank R. Donovan states that in 1963 a settlement was excavated in Newfoundland that seems to have been built during the time of Leif Eriksson's voyage. No one knows if Leif Eriksson himself lived in the house, however.

> [The remains] predate the voyage of Columbus by almost five hundred years. . . . [Dr. Helge Ingstad] discovered the ruins of nine structures and a primitive smithy near the fishing village of L'Anse aux Meadows. Only the remains of beaten earthen floors, the outlines of turf walls, and fireplaces with ember pits remain, plus some scraps of iron and a stone anvil. But one of the houses had a great hall in the Viking style, and the ember pits were typically Norse. The buildings were not structurally or stylistically similar to those built by Indians or Eskimos; furthermore, the natives had no knowledge of iron smelting.
>
> Modern techniques used to determine the age of artifacts indicate that the house was built around the year 1000. This coincides with the exact time that the sagas say Leif Eriksson discovered North America.

After the pioneering work done by the Vikings, the sailing ship developed fairly rapidly in northern Europe during the Middle Ages. We know, approximately, what the ships built in the eleventh and twelfth centuries looked like, because some are shown in the Bayeaux Tapestry. They were not unlike the Viking longships.[53]

One of the longships depicted on the tapestry was the *Mora,* which belonged to William the Conqueror. Naval authority Edwin Tunis describes it as a ship with a "high stem and stern post, the one rudder over the starboard side, the shields along the rail and the one square sail on a mast in the center of the ship."[54]

JUST HOW GOOD WERE THEY?

To determine whether the original design of the longship would have been seaworthy, several people and groups have attempted to reconstruct the ship. The earliest reconstruction took place in 1893. It was named *The Viking* and was sailed across the Atlantic by a Norwegian named Magnus Anderson. During the best day's sail, *The Viking* crossed a distance of 223 nautical miles. The captain and crew discovered the longship could travel at the same speed as a ship with two masts constructed in the nineteenth century, and it was easier to maneuver than the ships they were accustomed to sailing. As Anderson later recalled,

Since 1893 many replicas of the Viking longship have been made and tested for seaworthiness. Most of them performed admirably.

We noted with admiration the ship's graceful move-ments, and with pride we noted her speed, sometimes as much as eleven knots. . . .

The rudder is indeed a work of genius. In my experience the side rudder is much to be preferred in such a ship to a rudder on the stern-post; it worked satisfactorily in every way and had the advantage of never kicking, as a

LONDON BRIDGE IS FALLING DOWN

An unexpected reference to Vikings is found in a tune every English-speaking child knows. It refers to a battle fought by Saint Olaf of Norway, who had gone *i-viking* in his youth. In 1014 he helped King Athelred II of England take back London from the Danes who held it.

The saga, described in *The Vikings* by Frank R. Dono-van, draws a vivid picture of how the battle was won.

The Viking leader took his ships under London Bridge and wound cables round the stakes which supported the bridge, and taking the cables, they rowed all the ships downstream as hard as ever they could. The stakes were dragged along the bottom until they were loosed under the bridge . . . and the bridge came crashing down, and many fell into the river. . . . Now when the citizens saw that the River Thames was won, so that they could no longer pre-vent the ships from pressing up inland, they were stricken with terror at the advance of the ships and gave up the city.

The Anglo-Saxon chronicles, which were translated by Anne Savage, are strangely silent about this battle. The chronicle from the year of the attack states only that "the townsmen of London submitted and gave hostages, for they dreaded that he [Olaf] would fordo them." Viking im-plements of war have been recovered from the Thames around the site of the old bridge of London, indicating that the story told in the saga may be true. Whether it hap-pened exactly the way the saga told it, all children know the song that begins, "London Bridge is falling down."

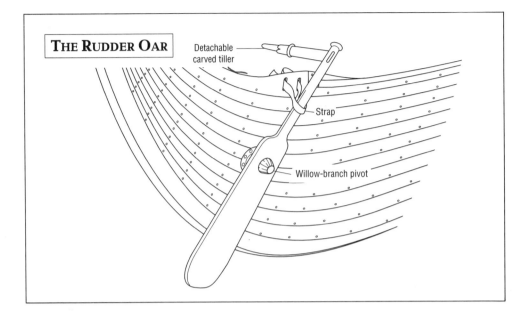

THE RUDDER OAR

Detachable carved tiller

Strap

Willow-branch pivot

stern-post rudder would certainly have done. One man could steer in any weather with merely a small line to help.[55]

Other replicas have been built, including one in 1963 by Danish Boy Scouts. They constructed a replica of an early Viking ship known as the Ladby ship, partly to see if horses could actually board the ship from a beach. The longship hull was relatively low to the water to make it easier for animals to jump out of or onto the ship. When loading or unloading began, the side of the hull was weighted to make it sit even lower in the water. Hale writes that

the sea trials of the Ladby ship were a complete success, with horses, scouts and hull all performing well. The ship proved surprisingly swift and handy on the open sea, again vindicating the skill and ingenuity of the Viking shipwrights.[56]

In 1991 a replica of the smaller Skuldelev longship was built. The *Helge Ask* proved that even with half the original crew number of twenty-four at the oars, the ship traveled swiftly in the water. The *Helge Ask* was found to have a working speed of nearly eight knots, proving a longship could have overtaken any other ship on the sea at the time. The sagas had already indicated this when a Viking named Gauti Tofason was said to have overtaken four Danish warships and would have captured a fifth one as well if a storm had not blown him off course. This speed made the longships formidable in battle.

AN INDIVIDUAL SPIRIT

The Vikings were formidable opponents and a strong presence wherever they went for another reason that had nothing to do

Scandinavian shipbuilders revolutionized sea travel when they built the longship. Their design inspired many of the ships that came long after the age of the Vikings came to an end.

with the longship. They had a strong sense of equality. Any Viking, from a chieftain to a *carl,* could own a longship if he had the money to build one, and he was free to sail it anywhere he chose. The Vikings did not seek treasure or conquest on behalf of a king or lord. They made their journeys to satisfy their own individual needs and desires.

Vikings felt a strong commitment to equality among men and freedom for individuals. Donovan sums up this commitment:

> When Rollo landed in France, his men were asked the name of their lord. They replied, "We have no lord, we are all equal." And after the feudal period, Normandy was the first French province to give up serfdom. Freedom and equality ultimately became the most important heritage of both France and England, and of the colonies they formed in America.[57]

The vehicle that allowed them the freedom to travel from country to country with their ideas and laws, the vehicle that carried their trade goods and colonists, was the longship.

 **NOTES**

Introduction
1. Gerald Simons and the Editors of Time-Life Books, *Barbarian Europe*. New York: Time-Life Books, 1968, p. 125.

Chapter 1: A Seafaring People
2. Quoted in Simons, *Barbarian Europe*, p. 125.
3. Frank R. Donovan, *The Vikings*. New York: American Heritage, 1964, p. 15.
4. Bertil Almgren, *The Viking*. Gothenburg, Sweden: Wahlstrom & Widstrand, 1967, p. 145.
5. Almgren, *The Viking*, p. 146.
6. Donovan, *The Vikings*, p. 19.
7. Almgren, *The Viking*, p. 143.
8. Donovan, *The Vikings*, p. 24.
9. Donovan, *The Vikings*, p. 24.
10. John Mills, *The Great Days of Sail*. Chicago: Follett, 1965, p. 8.
11. Mills, *The Great Days of Sail*, p. 10.

Chapter 2: Shipbuilding and Navigation
12. Almgren, *The Viking*, p. 248.
13. Peter Sawyer, ed., *The Oxford Illustrated History of the Vikings*. New York: Oxford University Press, 1997, p. 187.
14. Sawyer, *The Oxford Illustrated History of the Vikings*, p. 188.
15. Sawyer, *The Oxford Illustrated History of the Vikings*, p. 194.
16. Almgren, *The Viking*, p. 251.
17. Guy R. Williams, *The World of Model Ships and Boats*. New York: G. P. Putnam's Sons, 1971, p. 36.
18. Frank O. Braynard, *The Story of Ships*. New York: Grosset & Dunlap, 1962, p. 18.
19. Simons, *Barbarian Europe*, p. 144.
20. Almgren, *The Viking*, p. 11.
21. Almgren, *The Viking*, p. 11.
22. Quoted in Almgren, *The Viking*, p. 14.
23. Donovan, *The Vikings*, p. 94.

Chapter 3: Life at Sea
24. Eliot Wigginton, ed., *The Foxfire Book*, Garden City, NY: Anchor Books-Doubleday, 1972, p. 201.

25. Almgren, *The Viking*, p. 262.

26. Almgren, *The Viking*, p. 164.

27. Tony D. Triggs, *Viking Warriors.* New York: Bookwright Press, 1990, p. 20.

28. John Geipel, *Great Adventures of the Vikings.* New York: Rand McNally, 1977, p. 25.

29. Madeleine Pelner Cosman, *Fabulous Feasts: Medieval Cookery and Ceremony.* New York: George Braziller, 1976, p. 16.

Chapter 4: Exploration and Trade

30. John R. Hale, "The Viking Longship," *Scientific American,* vol. 278, no. 2, February 1998, p. 56.

31. Simons, *Barbarian Europe*, p. 128.

32. Simons, *Barbarian Europe*, p. 128.

33. Quoted in Donovan, *The Vikings*, p. 116.

34. Quoted in Donovan, *The Vikings*, p. 117.

35. Quoted in Donovan, *The Vikings*, p. 117.

36. Quoted in Donovan, *The Vikings*, p. 117.

Chapter 5: Warfare and Conquest

37. Quoted in Almgren, *The Viking*, p. 79.

38. Quoted in Anne Savage, *The Anglo-Saxon Chronicles.* England: Phoebe Phillips-Heinemann, Dorset Press, 1983, p. 73.

39. Quoted in Almgren, *The Viking*, p. 82.

40. Hale, "The Viking Longship," p. 57.

41. Hale, "The Viking Longship," p. 58.

42. Hale, "The Viking Longship," p. 63.

43. Donovan, *The Vikings*, p. 80.

44. Donovan, *The Vikings*, p. 37.

45. Quoted in Donovan, *The Vikings*, p. 38.

46. Quoted in Simons, *Barbarian Europe*, p. 131.

47. Quoted in Simons, *Barbarian Europe*, p. 131.

48. Quoted in Donovan, *The Vikings*, p. 148.

Chapter 6: The Viking Legacies

49. Donovan, *The Vikings*, p. 60.

50. Almgren, *The Viking*, p. 59.

51. Quoted in Almgren, *The Viking*, p. 105.

52. Almgren, *The Viking*, p. 105.

53. Williams, *The World of Model Ships and Boats*, p. 38.

54. Edwin Tunis, *Oars, Sails, and Steam.* Cleveland: World, 1952, p. 22.

55. Quoted in Almgren, *The Viking*, p. 254.

56. Hale, "The Viking Longship," pp. 62–63.

57. Donovan, *The Vikings*, p. 148.

Glossary

adze: A cutting tool that has a thin arched blade set at right angles to the handle and is used chiefly for shaping wood.

aft: To the rear or behind.

Althing: The legislative body made up of thirty-six (later thirty-nine) chiefs. The Althing created and upheld laws.

archipelago: An expanse of water with many scattered islands, or a group of islands.

berserk: Frenzied or crazed. A Viking warrior frenzied in battle and held to be invulnerable.

berserk gang: Berserk or uncontrollable fury.

bow: The forward part of a ship.

brynie* or *brynja: Chain mail.

cairn: A heap of stones piled up as a memorial or landmark.

cleat: A wedge-shaped piece fastened to or projecting from something and serving as a support or check. A wooden or metal fitting, usually with two projecting horns around which a rope may be made fast.

Danegeld: The gold paid to Danish Vikings to purchase a year of peace.

Danelaw: The parts of central and eastern England inhabited by and ruled by Danes.

deck: The floor in a ship.

fjord: A narrow inlet of sea between cliffs.

fore: To the front or forward.

halberd: A combination of battle ax and spear mounted on a handle about six feet long.

hawser: A large rope used for towing, mooring, or securing a ship.

hull: The main body of a ship.

inlet: A bay on the shore of a sea, lake or river, or a narrow water passage between peninsulas or through barrier islands leading to a bay or lagoon.

keel: A long timber extending along the center of the bottom of a ship, often projecting from the bottom.

kendtmand: "Man who knows," or a ship's pilot.

kloften: "The fork." A forked mast partner that held the mast in place on a keelson.

mast: A long pole or spar rising from the keel or deck of a ship and supporting the sail and rigging.

meginhufr: The rail board or gunwale of a ship. Also called a "strake." A line of planks that are joined together endwise from the stem to the stern of a ship.

prow: The pointed and projecting front of a ship.

redeless: Ill-advised.

reeve: A royal official with duties of overseeing the discharge of feudal obligations. A steward.

rigging: Lines and chains aboard a ship to support the sail and mast.

rowlock: An oarlock. A device to hold the oars in place.

scramasax: A narrow, single-edged sword of Frankish origin.

skald: A bard or storyteller. A wandering minstrel.

Skraelings: "Wretches." The Viking name for Indians or Eskimos.

sledges: Wooden wagons mounted on runners to glide over grass or snow.

spantrum: The spaces between the deck beams.

stem: Front end of a boat.

stern: Rear end of a boat.

sternpost: The principal member at the stern of a ship extending from keel to deck.

strake: A line of planks joined endwise from stem to stern.

thing: The local court or government in Scandinavia.

thwart: A seat where a man sits to row.

trenail: A wooden peg holding the rowlock in place.

vik: A bay or creek.

wadmal: Rough woolen cloth used for sails.

FOR FURTHER READING

Jan Adkins, *Wooden Ship.* Boston: Houghton Mifflin, 1978. A detailed account of how wooden ships were built in 1870.

Bertil Almgren, *The Viking.* Gothenburg, Sweden: Wahlstrom & Widstrand, 1967. A comprehensive history of Viking life and customs.

Frank R. Donovan, *The Vikings.* New York: American Heritage, 1964. A comprehensive look at Viking life.

Marguerite R. Duffy, *The Vikings.* Cleveland: World, 1965. An easy-to-understand account of Viking adventures.

John Geipel, *Great Adventures of the Vikings.* New York: Rand McNally, 1977. An easy-to-read account of Viking customs and adventures.

John Mills, *The Great Days of Sail.* Chicago: Follett, 1965. Describes how early sailing ships were made and how ships evolved through the centuries.

Marie Neurath, *The Vikings (They Lived Like This).* New York: Franklin Watts, 1970. A simply written history of Viking life.

Peter Sawyer, ed., *The Oxford Illustrated History of the Vikings.* New York: Oxford University Press, 1997. A detailed account of how the Vikings lived and how they built their longships.

Edwin Tunis, *Oars, Sails, and Steam.* Cleveland: World, 1952. A history of shipbuilding and the changes in how ships are propelled.

ADDITIONAL WORKS CONSULTED

Frank O. Braynard, *The Story of Ships*. New York: Grosset & Dunlap, 1962. A history of how ships were built and how they changed in design.

Lionel Casson et al., *Mysteries of the Past*. New York: American Heritage-Simon and Schuster, 1977. A compilation of unsolved mysteries throughout history, including the question of whether Vikings reached America before Columbus.

Madeleine Pelner Cosman, *Fabulous Feasts: Medieval Cookery and Ceremony*. New York: George Braziller, 1976. Describes how food was prepared and served from the time of the Saxon kings through the Middle Ages.

Eric R. Delderfield, *Kings and Queens of England and Great Britain*. Worcester, England: Trinity Press-Ebenezer Baylis & Son, 1975. Gives the dates and a brief description of the reigns of British monarchs.

John R. Hale, "The Viking Longship," *Scientific American*, vol. 278, no. 2, February 1998. An account of the history of Viking longships, how some of the ancient ships were found, and how some of the longships have been reconstructed.

Silver Ravenwolf, *To Ride a Silver Broomstick*. St. Paul: Llewellyn, 1993. A book about the religion of Wicca, which includes information about Viking gods.

Anne Savage, trans., *The Anglo-Saxon Chronicles*. England: Phoebe Phillips-Heinemann, Dorset Press, 1983. A discussion of the chronicles that were begun in the ninth century and listed yearly events from the days of pre-Roman Britain through most of the twelfth century.

Gerald Simons and the Editors of Time-Life Books, *Barbarian Europe*. New York: Time-Life Books, 1968. Part of the Time-Life "Great Ages of Man" series, this volume gives a capsulized account of the Viking Age.

Tony D. Triggs, *Viking Warriors*. New York: Bookwright Press, 1990. Covers Viking adventures and battles.

Eliot Wigginton, ed., *The Foxfire Book*. Garden City, NY: Anchor Books-Doubleday, 1972. An account of the people who live in the Appalachian mountains of America, showing that the mountaineers' methods of curing meat were similar to the methods used by the Vikings.

Guy R. Williams, *The World of Model Ships and Boats.* New York, G. P. Putnam's Sons, 1971. Tells how to build models of famous ships constructed throughout the centuries.

INDEX

PICTURE CREDITS

ABOUT THE AUTHOR

Lynda Trent has been writing novels for twenty years and has published fifty-three books. Among other achievements, she has been awarded the Rita by Romance Writers of America for *Opal Fires,* a contemporary mainstream romance novel. She has frequently been in the finals for both contemporary and historical romances for Ritas. In 1985 she won a bronze Porgy for best western novel from the West Coast Review of Books. She was honored as part of the Outstanding Historical Romance Writing Team for 1986. Translations of her fifty-three books are sold worldwide, and she has appeared on Burt Reynolds's TV show as well as on Geraldo Rivera's.